The Second Coming of CHRIST

The Second Coming of CHRIST

Charles SPURGEON

Whitaker House

Unless otherwise indicated, all Scripture quotations are taken from the *King James Version* (KJV) of the Bible.

Scripture quotations marked (RV) are taken from the *Revised Version* of the Holy Bible.

THE SECOND COMING OF CHRIST

ISBN: 0-88368-380-6
Printed in the United States of America
Copyright © 1996 by Whitaker House

Whitaker House
30 Hunt Valley Circle
New Kensington, PA 15068

3 4 5 6 7 8 9 10 11 12 13 / 06 05 04 03 02 01 00 99 98 97

Contents

Chapter One

He Is Coming with Clouds

Behold, he cometh with clouds; and every eye shall
see him, and they also which pierced him: and all
kindreds of the earth shall wail because of him.
Even so, Amen.
—Revelation 1:7

In reading the entire first chapter of Revelation, we observe how the beloved John saluted the seven churches in Asia with, *"Grace be unto you, and peace"* (v. 4). Blessed men scatter blessings. When the benediction of God rests upon us, we pour out benedictions upon others.

From this blessing, John's gracious heart rose into adoration of the great King of Kings. As the hymn puts it, "The holy to the holiest lead." They that are good at blessing men will be quick at blessing God.

It is a wonderful doxology that John has given us: *"Unto him that loved us, and washed us from our sins in his own blood, And hath made us kings and priests unto God and his Father; to him be glory and dominion for ever and ever. Amen"* (Revelation 1:5–6). I like the Revised Version for its alliteration in this case, although I cannot prefer it for other reasons. It reads: *"Unto him that loveth us, and loosed us from our sins by his blood"* (v. 5 RV). Truly our Redeemer has loosed us from sin, but the mention of His blood suggests washing rather than loosing. We can keep the alliteration and yet retain the meaning of cleansing if we read the passage, *"Unto him that loved us, and* laved *us." Loved* us, and *laved* us—carry those two words with you. Let them lie upon your tongue to sweeten your breath for prayer and praise. *"Unto him that loved us, and* laved *us...be glory and dominion for ever and ever."*

Then, John told of the dignity which the Lord has put upon us in making us kings and priests, and from this he ascribed royalty and dominion unto the Lord Himself. John had been extolling the great King, whom he called, *"the prince of the kings of the earth"* (v. 5). Such indeed He was, and is, and is to be (Revelation 4:8). When John had touched upon that royalty which is natural to our divine Lord, and that dominion which has come to Him by conquest and by the gift of the Father as the reward of all His travail, he then went on to note that Christ has *"made us kings."* Our Lord diffuses His royalty among His redeemed.

We praise Him because He is in Himself a king, and next, because He is a kingmaker, the fountain of honor and majesty. He has not only enough of royalty for Himself, but He hands a measure of His dignity to His people. He makes kings out of such common stuff as He finds in us poor sinners. Will we not adore Him for this? Will we not cast our crowns at His feet? He gave our crowns to us; will we not give them back to Him?

"To him be glory and dominion for ever and ever. Amen." King by divine nature! King by filial right! Kingmaker, lifting up the beggar from the dunghill to set him among princes! King of Kings by the unanimous love of all your crowned ones! *"Thou art he whom thy brethren shall praise"* (Genesis 49:8)! Reign forever! Unto You be hosannas of welcome and hallelujahs of praise. Lord of heaven and earth, let all things that are, or ever shall be, render unto You all glory in the highest.

Beloved, do not your souls catch fire as you think of the praises of Immanuel? Gladly would I fill the universe with His praises. "Oh, for a thousand tongues to sing" the glories of the Lord Jesus! If the Spirit who dictated the words of John has taken possession of our spirits, we will find adoration to be our highest delight. Never are we so near to heaven as when we are absorbed in the worship of Jesus, our Lord and God. Oh, that I could now adore Him as I will do when, delivered from this encumbering body, my soul will behold Him in the fullness of His glory!

It would seem from the chapter that John's adoration was increased by his expectation of the Lord's Second Coming, because he cries, *"Behold, he cometh with clouds."* John's adoration awoke his expectation, which all the while was lying in his soul as an element of the vehement heat of reverent love that he poured forth in his doxology. *"Behold, he cometh,"* he said, and thus he revealed one source of his reverence. *"Behold, he cometh,"*

9

and this exclamation was the result of his reverence. He adored until his faith realized his Lord and became a second and nobler sight.

I think, too, that his reverence was deepened and his adoration was rendered more fervent by his conviction of the speediness of his Lord's coming. *"Behold, he cometh,"* or is coming: John meant to assert that He is even now on His way. As workmen are moved to be more diligent in service when they hear their master's footfall, so saints are undoubtedly quickened in their devotion when they are conscious that He whom they worship is drawing near. He has gone away to the Father for a while, and so He has left us alone in this world; but He has said, *"I will come again, and receive you unto myself"* (John 14:3). We are confident that He will keep His word. Sweet is the remembrance of that loving promise.

That assurance was pouring its savor into John's heart while he was adoring. It became inevitable, as well as most right and proper, that his doxology at its close would have introduced him to the Lord Himself and caused him to cry out, *"Behold, he cometh."* Having worshipped among the pure in heart, he saw the Lord. Having adored the King, he saw Him assume the judgment seat and appear in the clouds of heaven.

When once we enter upon heavenly things, we know not how far we can go nor how high we can climb. John, who began with blessing the churches, now beholds his Lord. May the Holy Spirit help us to think reverently of the wondrous coming of our blessed Lord, when He will appear to the delight of His people and the dismay of the ungodly!

There are three points I would like to glean from the text. They will seem commonplace to some of you. Indeed, they are the commonplace of our divine faith, yet nothing can be of greater importance. The first is that our Lord Jesus is coming: *"Behold, he cometh with clouds."* The second is that Christ's coming will be seen by all: *"Every eye shall see him, and they also which pierced him."* Finally, this coming will cause great sorrow: *"All kindreds of the earth shall wail because of him."*

THE LORD JESUS CHRIST IS COMING AGAIN

May the Holy Spirit help us as we remember that our Lord Jesus Christ is coming! This announcement is thought worthy of a note of admiration. As the Latins would say, there is an *Ecce* placed here: *"Behold, he cometh."* As in the old books the printers put hands in the margin pointing to special passages, such is this *"Behold!"* It is a *Nota Bene,* calling upon us to note well what we are reading. Here is something that we are to hold and behold. We now hear a voice crying, "Come and see!" The Holy Spirit never uses superfluous words or redundant notes of exclamation: when He cries, *"Behold,"* it is because there is reason for deep and lasting attention.

Will you turn away when He bids you pause and ponder, linger and look? You who have been beholding vanity, come and behold the fact that Jesus comes. You who have been beholding this and looking at that and thinking of nothing worthwhile, forget these passing sights and spectacles, and for once behold a scene which has no parallel. It is not a monarch in her jubilee, but the King of Kings in His glory. *"This same Jesus"* (Acts 1:11) who went up from Olivet into heaven is coming again to earth in like manner as His disciples saw Him go up into heaven. Come and behold this great sight. If ever there were a thing in the world worth looking at, it is this. Behold! See if there were ever glory like unto His glory!

Hearken to the midnight cry, *"Behold, the bridegroom cometh!"* (Matthew 25:6). It has practical implications for you. *"Go ye out to meet him"* (Matthew 25:6). This voice is to you, O sons of men. Do not carelessly turn aside, for the Lord God Himself demands your attention. He commands you to *"Behold!"* Will you be blind when God bids you to behold? Will you shut your eyes when your Savior cries, *"Behold"*? When the finger of inspiration points the way, will not your eyes follow where it directs you? *"Behold, he cometh."* O beloved, look here, I implore you.

A Vivid Realization

If we read the words of our text carefully, this *"Behold"* shows us first that this coming is to be vividly realized. I think I see John. He is in the spirit, but suddenly he seems startled into a keener and more solemn attention. His mind is more awake than usual, though he was always a man of bright eyes that saw afar. (We compare him to the eagle for the height of his flight and the keenness of his vision.) Yet, all of a sudden, even he seemed startled with a more astounding vision. He cried out, "Behold! Behold!" He has caught sight of his Lord. He said not, "He will come by and by," but, "I can see Him; He is now coming." He had evidently realized the Second Advent. He had so conceived of the Second Coming of the Lord that it had become a matter of fact to him, a matter to be spoken of and even to be written down. *"Behold, he cometh!"*

Have you and I ever realized the coming of Christ so fully as this? Perhaps we believe that He will come. I should hope that we all do. If we believe that the Lord Jesus has come the first time, we believe also that He will come the second time. But, are these equally assured truths to us? Perhaps we have vividly realized the first appearing from Bethlehem to Golgotha, and we have traced the Lord from Calvary to Olivet, understanding that blessed cry, *"Behold the Lamb of God, which taketh away the sin of the world!"* (John 1:29). Yes, *"the Word was made flesh, and dwelt among us, (and we beheld his glory, the glory as of the only begotten of the Father,) full of grace and truth"* (John 1:14). But, have we with equal firmness grasped the thought that He will *"appear the second time without sin unto salvation"* (Hebrews 9:28)? Do we now say to each other when we gather in happy fellowship, "Yes, our Lord is coming"?

His coming should be to us not only a prophecy assuredly believed among us, but a scene that is pictured in our souls and anticipated in our hearts. My imagination has often set forth that awesome scene; but better still, my faith has realized it. I have heard the chariot wheels of the Lord's approach, and I have endeavored to set my house in order for His reception. I have felt the shadow of the great cloud that will attend Him damping the ardor of my worldliness. I hear even now in my spirit the sound of the last trumpet, whose tremendous blast startles my soul to serious action and puts force into my life. I pray to God that I would live more completely under the influence of that stately event!

Brothers and sisters, to this realization I invite you. One of Christ's followers said to his friends after the Lord had risen, *"The Lord is risen indeed"* (Luke 24:34). I want you to feel just as certain that the Lord is coming indeed. I desire that, as we meet our fellow Christians, we would say to one another, *"Behold, he cometh!"* We are sure that He will come and that He is on the way, but the benefit of a more vivid realization would be incalculable.

A Zealous Proclamation

This coming is to be zealously proclaimed, for John did not just calmly say, *"He cometh,"* but he vigorously cried, *"Behold, he cometh!"* Just as the herald of a king prefaces his message by a trumpet blast that calls attention, so John cries, *"Behold!"* As the town crier of old was accustomed to saying, "O yes! O yes!" or to use some other striking formula by which he called on men to pay attention to his announcement, so John has stood in the midst of us and cried, *"Behold, he cometh!"* He called attention by that emphatic word, *"Behold!"* It was no ordinary message that John brought, and he would not have us treat his word as a commonplace saying. He threw his heart into the announcement. He proclaimed it loudly, he proclaimed it solemnly, and he proclaimed it with authority: *"Behold, he cometh."*

A Frequent Proclamation

Beloved, no truth ought to be more frequently proclaimed, next to the first coming of the Lord, than His Second Coming. You cannot thoroughly set forth all the ends and bearings of the first advent if you forget the second. At the Lord's Supper, there is no discerning the Lord's body unless you discern His first coming, but there is no drinking of His cup to its fullness unless you hear Him say, *"Till I come"* (Revelation 2:25). You must look forward as well as backward.

So must it be with all our ministries; we must look to Christ on the cross and on the throne. We must vividly realize that He, who has once come, is coming again, or else our testimonies will be marred and one-sided. We will make lame work of preaching and teaching if we leave out either advent.

An Assuring Proclamation

Next, this truth is to be unquestionably asserted. *"Behold, he cometh."* It is not, "Perhaps He will come," or, "Possibly He may yet appear." *"Behold, he cometh"* should be dogmatically asserted as an absolute certainty, which has been realized by the heart of the man who proclaims it.

All the prophets said that He will come. From Enoch down to the last that spoke by inspiration, they declared, *"Behold, the Lord cometh with ten thousands of his saints"* (Jude 1:14). You will not find one who has spoken by the authority of God who does not, either directly or by implication, assert the coming of the Son of Man, when the multitudes born of woman will be summoned to His bar to receive the recompense of their deeds. All the promises are travailing with this prophecy: *"Behold, he cometh."*

We have His own word for it, and this makes assurance doubly sure. He has told us that He will come again. He often assured His disciples that if He went away from them, He would come again to them (John 14:28). He left us the Lord's Supper as a parting token to be observed until He comes (1 Corinthians 11:26). As often as we break bread, we are reminded of the fact that, though it is a most blessed ordinance, yet it is a temporary one that will cease to be celebrated when our absent Lord is once again present with us.

What, dear ones, is there to hinder Christ from coming? When I have studied and thought over this word, *"Behold, he cometh,"* I have said to myself, Yes, indeed He does: who could hold Him back? His heart is with His church on earth. In the place where He fought the battle, He desires to celebrate the victory. His *"delights* [are] *with the sons of men"* (Proverbs 8:31). He and all His saints are waiting for the day of His appearing. The very earth, in her sorrow and her groaning, travails for His coming (Romans 8:22), which is to be her redemption. The creation is made subject to vanity for a little while; but when the Lord comes again, the creation itself also *"shall be delivered from the bondage of corruption into the glorious liberty of the children of God"* (Romans 8:21).

We might question whether He would come a second time if He had not already come the first time. However, if He came to Bethlehem, be assured that His feet will yet stand upon Olivet. If He came to die, doubt not that He will come to reign. If He came to be *"despised and rejected of men"* (Isaiah 53:3), why should we doubt that *"He shall come...to be admired in all them that believe"* (2 Thessalonians 1:10)? His sure coming is to be unquestionably asserted.

An Attention-Demanding Proclamation

Dear friends, this fact that He will come again is to be taught as demanding our immediate interest. *"Behold, he cometh with clouds."* Behold, look at it, meditate on it. It is worth thinking of. It concerns you personally. Study it again and again. *"He cometh."* He will so soon be here that it is put in the present tense: *"He cometh."* That shaking of the earth, that blotting out of sun and moon, that fleeing of heaven and earth before His face—all these are so nearly here that John described them as accomplished. *"Behold, he cometh."*

17

There is a sense hovering in the background that Christ is already on the way. All that He is doing in providence and grace is a preparation for His coming. All the events of human history, all the great decisions of His stately majesty whereby He rules all things—all these are tending towards the day of His appearing. Do not think that He delays His coming and then suddenly He will rush here in hot haste. He has arranged for it to take place as soon as wisdom allows. We know not what may make the present delay imperative, but the Lord knows, and that suffices.

You grow uneasy because nearly two thousand years have passed since His Ascension and Jesus has not yet come; but you do not know what had to be arranged for and how much a lapse of time was absolutely necessary for the Lord's designs. Those are no little matters which have filled up the great pause: the intervening centuries have teemed with wonders. A thousand things may have been necessary in heaven itself before the consummation of all things could be arrived at. When our Lord comes, it will be seen that He came as quickly as He could in His infinite wisdom. He cannot behave Himself otherwise than wisely, perfectly, divinely. He cannot be moved by fear or passion so as to act hastily as you and I too often do. He dwells in the leisure of eternity and in the serenity of omnipotence. He does not have to measure out days, months, and years and to accomplish so much in such a space or else leave His life's work undone. Rather, according to the power of an endless life, He proceeds steadily on. To Him a thousand years are but as one day (2 Peter 3:8). Therefore, be assured that the Lord is even now coming. He is making everything tend that way. All things are working towards that grand climax. At this moment, and every moment since He went away, the Lord Jesus has been coming back again. *"Behold, he cometh!"* He is on the way! He is nearer every hour!

A Manifest Proclamation

And we are told that His coming will be attended by a peculiar sign: *"Behold, he cometh with clouds."* We will have no need to question whether it is the Son of Man who has come or whether He is indeed come. This is to be no secret matter: His coming will be as manifest as yonder clouds. In the wilderness the presence of Jehovah was known by a visible pillar of cloud by day and an equally visible pillar of fire by night (Exodus 13:21–22). That pillar of cloud was the sure token that the Lord was in His Holy Place, dwelling between the cherubim. Such is the token of the coming of the Lord Jesus Christ.

> Every eye the cloud shall scan,
> Ensign of the Son of man.

It is written, *"And then shall appear the sign of the Son of man in heaven: and then shall all the tribes of the earth mourn, and they shall see the Son of man coming in the clouds of heaven with power and great glory"* (Matthew 24:30). I cannot quote at this time all the passages of Scripture in which it is indicated that our Lord will come either sitting upon a cloud (Revelation 14:14, 15, 16), or *"with clouds,"* or *"in the clouds of heaven,"* but such expressions are abundant. Is it not to show that His coming will be majestic? He makes the clouds His chariots. He comes with hosts of attendants, and these of a nobler sort than earthly monarchs can summon to do them homage.

With clouds of angels, cherubim, seraphim, and all the armies of heaven, He comes. With all the forces of nature, thundercloud, and blackness of tempest, the Lord of all makes His triumphant entrance to judge the world. The clouds are the dust of His feet in that terrible day of battle when He will rid Himself of His adversaries, shaking them out of the earth with His thunder, and consuming them with the devouring flame of His lightning. All of heaven will gather with its utmost pomp at the great appearing of the Lord, and all the terrible grandeur of nature will then be seen at its fall. Not as the Man of Sorrows, despised and rejected of men, will Jesus come. Rather, as Jehovah came upon Sinai in the midst of thick clouds and a terrible darkness, so will He come, whose coming will be the final judgment.

A Mighty Proclamation

The clouds are meant to set forth the might, as well as the majesty, of His coming. *"Ascribe ye strength unto God: his excellency is over Israel, and his strength is in the clouds"* (Psalm 68:34).

This was the royal token given by Daniel the prophet: *"I saw in the night visions, and, behold, one like the Son of man came with the clouds of heaven"* (Daniel 7:13). Not less than divine is the glory of the Son of God, who once had nowhere to lay His head. The most sublime objects in nature will most aptly minister to the manifest glory of the returning King. *"Behold, he cometh,"* not with the swaddling cloths of His infancy, the weariness of His manhood, or the shame of His death, but with all the glorious tapestry of heaven's high chambers. The hangings of the divine throne room will aid His stately entrance.

A Terrifying Proclamation

The clouds also denote the terror of His coming to the ungodly. His saints will be caught up together with Him in the clouds, to meet the Lord in the air (1 Thessalonians 4:17); but the clouds will turn their blackness and horror of darkness to those that remain on earth. Then will the impenitent behold this dread vision: *"the Son of man coming in the clouds of heaven."* The clouds will fill them with dread, and the dread will be abundantly justified, for those clouds are big with vengeance and will burst in judgment on their heads. His Great White Throne, though it is bright and lustrous with hope for His people, will, with its very brightness and whiteness of immaculate justice, strike dead the hopes of all those who trusted that they might live in sin and yet go unpunished. *"Behold, he cometh with clouds."*

I am in happy circumstances at present because my subject requires no effort of imagination from me. To indulge on such a theme would be a wretched desecration of so sublime a subject that should come home to all hearts in its own simplicity. Think clearly for a moment until the meaning becomes real to you. Jesus Christ is coming in unmatched, majestic splendor. When He comes, He will be enthroned far above the attacks of His enemies, the persecutions of the godless, and the sneers of skeptics. He is coming in the clouds of heaven, and we will be among the witnesses of His appearing. Let us dwell on this truth.

EVERYONE WILL SEE HIS APPEARING

My second observation about the text is that our Lord's coming will be seen by all. *"Behold, he cometh with clouds; and every eye shall see him, and they also which pierced him."* To my way of thinking, the word *every* allows no exceptions, leaving no one excluded. *"Every eye shall see him."*

By Physical Eyes

First, I gather from this expression that it will be a literal appearing and an actual sight. If the Second Advent were to be a spiritual manifestation to be perceived by the minds of men, the phraseology would have been, "Every mind shall perceive him." But it is not so; we read, *"Every eye shall see him."* Now, the mind can behold the spiritual, but the eye can only see that which is distinctly material and visible. The Lord Jesus Christ will not come spiritually, for in that sense He is already here; but He will come really and substantially, for *"every eye shall see him,"* even those unspiritual eyes that gazed on Him with hate and pierced Him. Do not dreamily say to yourself, "Oh, there is some spiritual meaning about all this." Do not destroy the teaching of the Holy Spirit by the idea that there will be a spiritual manifestation of the Christ of God, but that a literal appearing is out of the question. That would be altering the record. The Lord Jesus will come to earth a second time as literally as He has come a first time. The same Christ who ate a piece of honeycomb and of broiled fish after He had risen from the dead; the same Jesus who said, *"Handle me, and see; for a spirit hath not flesh and bones, as ye see me have"* (Luke 24:39)—*"this same Jesus...in like manner"* (Acts 1:11), with a material body, is to come in the clouds of heaven. In the same manner as He went up, He will come down. He will be literally seen. The words cannot be honestly read in any other way.

"Every eye shall see him." Yes, I do literally expect to see my Lord Jesus with these eyes of mine, even as that saint Job expected, who long ago fell asleep, believing that *"though after my skin worms destroy this body, yet in my flesh shall I see God"* (Job 19:26). He believed his eyes, and not another's, would see for himself. There will be a real resurrection of the body—though the moderns doubt it—such that we will see Jesus with our own eyes. We will not find ourselves in a shadowy,

dreamy land of floating fictions where we may perceive but cannot see. We will not be airy nothings—mysterious, vague, and impalpable. Rather, we will literally see our glorious Lord, whose appearing will be no phantom show or shadow dance. Never a day will be more real than the Day of Judgment; never a sight will be more true than the Son of Man upon the throne of His glory. Will you take this statement to heart so that you may feel the force of it? We are getting too far away from facts nowadays and too much into the realm of myths and notions. *"Every eye shall see him."* In this there will be no delusion.

By All Kinds of Eyes

Note well that He is to be seen by all kinds of men: *"Every eye shall see him"*—the king and the peasant, the most learned and the most ignorant. Those who were blind before will see when He appears. I remember a man born blind who loved our Lord most intensely, and he was happy to glory in this, that his eyes had been reserved for his Lord. Said he, "The first whom I shall ever see will be the Lord Jesus Christ. The first sight that greets my newly-opened eyes will be the Son of Man in His glory." There is great comfort in this to all who are now unable to behold the sun. Since *"every eye shall see him,"* you also will see the King in His beauty.

Small pleasure is this to eyes that are full of filthiness and pride. You care not for this sight, and yet you must see it whether you please or do not please. You have hitherto shut your eyes to good things, but you must see Him when He comes. All that dwell upon the face of the earth—if not all at the same moment, yet still with the same certainty—will behold the once crucified Lord. They will not be able to hide themselves nor to hide Him from their eyes. They will dread the sight, but it will come upon them, even as the sun shines on the thief who delights in the darkness. They will be obliged to own in dismay that they behold the Son of Man. So overwhelmed with the sight, they will not be able to deny it.

He will be seen of those who have been long since dead. What a sight that will be for Judas, for Pilate, for Caiaphas, and for Herod! What a sight it will be for those who, in the course of their lives, said that there was no Savior and no need of one, or that Jesus was a mere man and His blood was not a propitiation for sin! Those that scoffed and reviled Him have long since died, but they will all rise again to this heritage among the rest: they will see Him whom they blasphemed sitting in the clouds of heaven.

Prisoners are troubled at the sight of the judge. The trumpet of the court brings no music to the ears of criminals. But you must hear it, O impenitent sinners! Even in your graves you must hear the voice of the Son of God and live and come forth from the tombs to receive the things done in your bodies, whether they were good or bad (2 Corinthians 5:10). Death cannot hide you, nor can the vault conceal you, nor will rottenness and corruption deliver you. You are bound to see with your own eyes the Lord who will judge both you and your fellowmen.

By Eyes That Pierced Him

It is emphasized in the text that He will be seen by *"they also which pierced him."* In this are included all of the company who nailed Him to the tree, along with those who took the spear and made the gash in His side—indeed, all that had a hand in His cruel crucifixion. It includes all of these, but it encompasses many more besides. *"They also which pierced him"* are by no means a few.

Who have pierced Him? Why, those that once professed to love Him and have gone back to the world. Those that once ran well, what has hindered them (Galatians 5:7)? Now they use their tongues to speak against the Christ whom once they professed to love. They whose inconsistent lives have brought dishonor upon the sacred name of Jesus have also pierced Him. Those who refused His love, stifled their consciences, and refused His rebukes also have pierced Him. Alas, so many of you are piercing Him now by your base neglect of His salvation! They who have gone every Sunday to hear of Him but have remained *"hearers only, deceiving* [them]*selves"* (James 1:22), destroying their own souls rather than yield to His infinite love, have pierced His tender heart.

Dear ones, I wish I could plead effectively with you so that you would not continue any longer among the number of those that pierced Him. If you will look at Jesus now and mourn for your sin,

26

He will put your sin away. Then you will not be ashamed to see Him in that day. Even though you did pierce Him, you will be able to sing, *"Unto him that loved us, and washed us from our sins in his own blood"* (Revelation 1:5). But remember, if you persevere in piercing Him and fighting against Him, you will still have to see Him in that day to your terror and despair. He will be seen by you and by me, however badly we may behave. And what horror will that sight cost us!

I am often ill; who knows how soon I will come to my end? I would use all that remains to me of physical strength and providential opportunity to spread the Gospel. We never know how soon we may be cut off, and then we are gone forever from the opportunity of benefiting our fellowmen. It would be a pity to be taken away with one opportunity of doing good left unused. Thus, I earnestly plead with you under the shadow of this great truth: I urge you to be ready, since we will both behold the Lord in the day of His appearing. Yes, I will stand in that great throng. You also will be there. How will you feel? You are not accustomed, perhaps, to attend a place of worship, but you will be there. The occasion will be very solemn to you. You may absent yourself from the assemblies of the saints now, but you will not be able to absent yourself from the gathering of that day. You will be there, one in that great multitude. You will see Jesus the Lord as truly as if you were the only person before Him, and He will look upon you as certainly as if you were the only one who had been summoned to His bar.

Kindly think about this. Let your heart dwell on it. Silently repeat to yourself the words, *"Every eye shall see him, and they also which pierced him."*

HIS COMING WILL BRING SORROW

My third comment on this text is a painful one, but it needs to be enlarged upon: His coming will cause great sorrow. What does the text say about His coming? *"All kindreds of the earth shall wail because of him."*

A General Sorrow

"All kindreds of the earth." Thus, this sorrow will be very general. You thought, perhaps, that when Christ came, He would come to a glad world, welcoming Him with song and music. You may have thought that there might be a few ungodly people who would be destroyed with the breath of His mouth, but that the bulk of mankind would receive Him with delight. See how different it will be: *"all kindreds of the earth"*—all sorts of men that belong to the earth, all earthborn men, men out of all nations, kindreds, and tongues. They will weep and wail and gnash their teeth at His coming. Oh, what a sad outlook! There are no smooth things to prophesy. What do you think of this?

A Great Sorrow

Next, this sorrow will be very great. They will *"wail."* I cannot put into English the full meaning

28

of that most expressive word. Sound it out at length, and it conveys its own meaning. It is as when men wring their hands and burst out into a loud cry, or as when eastern women in their anguish rend their garments and lift up their voices with the most mournful notes. *"All kindreds of the earth shall wail,"* wail as a mother laments over her dead child, wail as a man might wail who found himself hopelessly imprisoned and doomed to die. Such will be the hopeless grief of all the kindreds of the earth at the sight of Christ in the clouds. If they remain impenitent, they will not be able to be silent; they will not be able to repress or conceal their anguish. Rather, they will wail and openly give vent to their horror. What a sound that will be that will go up before high heaven when Jesus sits upon the cloud and in the fullness of His power summons them to judgment! Then they *"shall wail because of him."*

Will your voice be heard in that wailing? Will your heart be breaking in that general dismay? How will you escape? If you are one of the *"kindreds of the earth"* and remain impenitent, you will wail with the rest of them. Unless you now fly to Christ, hide yourself in Him, and so become one of the kindred of heaven; unless you repent and become one of His chosen, blood-washed ones who will praise His name for washing them from their sins, there will be wailing at the judgment seat of Christ, and you will be in it.

From this text it becomes quite clear that men will not be universally converted when Christ comes, because, if they were so, they would not wail. Then, they would lift up the cry, "Welcome, Son of God!" The coming of Christ would be as the hymn puts it:

Hark, those bursts of acclamation!
Hark, those loud triumphant chords!
Jesus takes the highest station.
Oh, what joy the sight affords!

These acclamations come from His people. But according to the text, the multitude of mankind will weep and wail, and therein they will not be among His people. Do not, therefore, look for salvation at some future day, but believe in Jesus now, and find in Him your Savior at once. If you joy in Him now, you will much more rejoice in Him in that day; but if you will have cause to wail at His coming, it will be well to wail at once.

False Expectations

Note one more truth. It is quite certain that when Jesus comes in these latter days, men will not be expecting great things of Him. You know the talk nowadays about "a larger hope." Those who put forth this vain philosophy deceive the people with the idle dream of repentance and restoration after death, a fiction unsupported by the least bit of Scripture. If the kindreds of the earth expected that they would die out and cease to be when Christ comes, they would be rejoicing because they had escaped the wrath of God instead of wailing. Would not each unbeliever say, "It were a consummation devoutly to be wished"? If they thought that at His coming there would be a universal restoration and a general delivery of souls long shut up in prison, would they wail? If Jesus were supposed to come to proclaim a general restoration, they would not wail but would shout for joy.

Because His coming to the impenitent is ominous with black despair, they will wail because of Him. If His first coming did not give you eternal life, His Second Coming will not. If you did not hide in His wounds when He came as your Savior, there will be no hiding place for you when He comes as your Judge. They will weep and wail because, having rejected the Lord Jesus, they have turned their backs on the last possibility of hope.

Why do they *"wail because of him"*? Will it not be because they will see Him in His glory and they will recollect that they slighted and despised Him? They will see Him come to judge them, as they remember that once He stood at their door with mercy in His hands and said, "Open to me," but they would not admit Him. They refused His blood; they refused His righteousness; they trifled with His sacred name; now, they must give an account for this wickedness. They put Him away in scorn; now, when He comes, they find that they can trifle with Him no longer. The days of child's play and of foolish delay are over; now, they have solemnly to give an accounting of their lives. See, the books are opened! They are covered with dismay as they remember their sins and know that they are written down by a faithful pen. They must give an account. Unwashed and unforgiven, they cannot render that account without knowing that the sentence will be, *"Depart from me, ye cursed"* (Matthew 25:41). This is why they weep and wail because of Him.

O souls, my natural love of ease makes me wish that I could present pleasant things to you, but they are not in my commission. However, I scarcely need to wish to put forth a soft Gospel, for so many are already doing it to you at your cost. Since I love your immortal souls, I dare not flatter you. As I will have to answer for it in the last great day, I must tell you the truth.

> Ye sinners, seek His face,
>   Whose wrath you cannot bear.

Seek the mercy of God right now. Although I am in pain, I have written this to implore you to be reconciled to God. *"Kiss the Son, lest he be angry, and ye perish from the way, when his wrath is kindled but a little. Blessed are all they that put their trust in him"* (Psalm 2:12).

However, if you will not have my Lord Jesus, He is coming all the same. He is on the road now, and when He comes, you *"shall wail because of him."* Oh, that you would make Him your friend, and then meet Him with joy! Why would you choose eternal death? He gives life to all those who trust Him. Believe, and live.

May God save your souls right now, and He will have the glory. Amen.

Chapter Two

The Reward of the Righteous

When the Son of man shall come in his glory,
and all the holy angels with him,
then shall he sit upon the throne of his glory:
And before him shall be gathered all nations:
and he shall separate them one from another,
as a shepherd divideth his sheep from the goats:
And he shall set the sheep on his right hand,
but the goats on the left.
Then shall the King say unto them on his right hand,
Come, ye blessed of my Father, inherit the kingdom
prepared for you from the foundation of the world:
For I was an hungered, and ye gave me meat:
I was thirsty, and ye gave me drink:
I was a stranger, and ye took me in:
Naked, and ye clothed me:
I was sick, and ye visited me:
I was in prison, and ye came unto me.
—Matthew 25:31–36

To mount above this present evil world to something nobler and better is exceedingly beneficial to our souls. *"The cares of this world, and the deceitfulness of riches"* (Mark 4:19) are apt to choke everything good within us, and we grow fretful and despondent, perhaps proud and carnal. It is well for us to cut down these thorns and briars, because heavenly seed sown among them is not likely to yield a harvest. I do not know a better sickle with which to cut them down than thoughts of the kingdom to come.

In the valleys in Switzerland, many of the inhabitants are deformed and dwarfish, all of them having a sickly appearance, because the atmosphere is permeated with noxious vapors and is close and stagnant. You traverse them as rapidly as you can and are glad to escape from them. Up in the mountains you will find a hardy race who breathe the clear, fresh air as it blows from the virgin snows of the Alpine summits. It would be well for their frames if the dwellers in the valleys could frequently leave their abodes among the marshes and the fever mists and could get themselves up into the clear atmosphere above.

It is to such an exploit of climbing that I invite you now. May the Spirit of God bear us upon eagles' wings so that we may leave the mists of fear, the fevers of anxiety, and all the ills that gather in this valley of earth, and get ourselves up to the mountains of future joy and blessedness where it is to be our delight to dwell forever, world without end! May God disentangle us now for a little while, cut the cords that keep us here below, and permit us to mount! Some of us are like chained eagles fastened to the rocks; however, unlike the eagles, we begin to love our chains and would, if it really came to the test, be afraid to have them snapped.

If our bodies cannot at once escape from the chains of mortal life, yet may God grant us grace that our spirits may escape. Leaving the body like a servant at the foot of the hill, may our souls, like Abraham, go to the top of the mountain and have communion with the Most High.

While examining this text, I direct your attention, first, to the circumstances which surround the rewarding of the righteous; secondly, to their portion; and thirdly, to the inheritors themselves.

CIRCUMSTANCES OF OUR REWARD

We read, *"When the Son of man shall come in his glory."* It appears that we must not expect to receive our reward until by-and-by. Like the hireling, we must fulfill our day, and then at evening we will have our pay. Too many Christians look for a present reward for their labors. If they meet with success, they begin doting upon it as though they had received their recompense. Like the disciples who returned saying, *"Lord, even the devils are subject unto us"* (Luke 10:17), they rejoice too exclusively in present prosperity; whereas the Master bade them not to look upon miraculous success as being their reward since that might not always be the case. Christ said, *"Notwithstanding in this rejoice not, that the spirits are subject unto you; but rather rejoice, because your names are written in heaven"* (Luke 10:20).

Success in the ministry is not the Christian minister's true reward. It is an earnest, a pledge, but the wages still wait. You must not look on the esteem of your fellowmen as being the reward of excellence, because often you will meet with the reverse: you will find your best actions misconstrued and your motives misinterpreted. If you are looking for your reward here, I may warn you of the apostle's words: *"If in this life only we have hope in Christ, we are of all men most miserable"* (1 Corinthians 15:19). Other men get their rewards in the present. Even the Pharisee gets his— *"Verily I say unto you, They have their reward"* (Matthew 6:2, 5, 16)—but we have none here.

To be despised and rejected of men is the Christian's lot. Even among his fellow Christians, he will not always stand in good repute. It is not unqualified kindness or total love that we receive, even from the saints. If you look to Christ's bride herself for your reward, you will miss it. If you expect to receive your crown from the hand of your brothers in the ministry who know your labors and who ought to sympathize with your trials, you will be mistaken. *"When the Son of man shall come in his glory"* is your time of recompense—not today, tomorrow, or at any time in this world. Reckon nothing that you acquire, no honor that you gain, to be the reward of your service to your Master; that dividend is reserved for the time *"when the Son of man shall come in his glory."*

Observe with delight the majestic person by whose hand the reward is given. It is written, *"When the* [King] *shall come."* Beloved, we love the King's court attendants; we delight to be numbered with them ourselves. It is no mean thing to do service to Him whose head,

> Though once 'twas crowned with thorns,
> Is crowned with glory now.

However, it is a delightful thought that the service of rewarding us will not be left to the courtiers. The angels will be there, and the beloved of the King will be there; but heaven was not prepared by them, nor can it be given by them. Their hands will not yield us a coronation. We will join their songs, but their songs will not be our reward. We will bow with them, and they with us. However, it will not be possible for them to give us the recompense of the reward: that starry crown is all too weighty for an angel's hand to bring, and the benediction all too sweet to be pronounced even by celestial lips. The King Himself must say, *"Well done, good and faithful servant"* (Matthew 25:23).

What do you say to this, my dear one? You have felt a temptation to look to God's servants, to the approval of the minister, to the kindly look of parents, to the word of commendation from your coworker. All these you value—and I do not blame you—but these may fail you. Therefore, never consider them as being the reward. You must wait until the time when the King comes. Then it will neither be your brothers, your pastors, your parents, nor your helpers, but the King Himself who will say to you, *"Come, ye blessed."*

How this sweetens heaven! It will be Christ's own gift. How this makes the benediction doubly blessed! It will come from His lips, which drop like myrrh and flow with honey. Beloved, it is Christ who became a curse for us who will give the blessing to us. Roll this as a sweet morsel around your tongues.

The character in which our Lord Jesus will appear is significant. Jesus will truly then be revealed as *"the King."* *"Then shall the King say..."* It was to Him as King that the service was rendered, and it is from Him as King that the reward must therefore come. Thus, upon the very threshold of His return, questions of self-examination arise: Since the King will not reward the servants of another prince, am I therefore His servant? Is it my joy to wait at the threshold of His gates and sit like Mordecai at the courts of Ahasuerus, at the entrance of His door? Say, soul, do you serve the King? My meaning here is not the kings and queens of earth—let them have loyal servants for their subjects—but saints are servants of the Lord Jesus Christ, the King of Kings. Are you one? If you are not, when the King comes in His glory, there can be no reward for you.

I long in my own heart to recognize Christ's kingly office more than I have ever done. It has been my delight to preach Christ dying on the cross, for *"God forbid that I should glory, save in the cross of our Lord Jesus Christ"* (Galatians 6:14). However, for myself I want to realize Him on His throne, reigning in my heart, having a right to do as He wills with me. I want to be in the condition of Abraham, who, when God spoke—though it was to tell him to offer up his own Isaac—never asked a question but simply said, *"Here am I"* (Genesis 22:11). Beloved, seek to know and feel the controlling power of the King; for else, when He comes, since you have not known Him as King, He cannot know you as servant. It is only to the servant that the King can give the reward that is spoken of in this text.

Now, let's move on. *"When the Son of man shall come in his glory."* The fullness of this is impossible to conceive.

> Imagination's utmost stretch
> In wonder dies away.

However, this we know—and it is the sweetest thing we can know—that if we have been partakers with Jesus in His shame, we also will be sharers with Him in the luster which will surround Him. Are you, beloved, one with Christ Jesus? Are you of His flesh and of His bones? Does a vital union knit you to Him? Then you are today with Him in His shame; you have taken up His cross and gone with Him *"without the camp, bearing his reproach"* (Hebrews 13:13). Undoubtedly, you will be with Him when the cross is exchanged for the crown. But judge yourself: if you are not with Him in the regeneration, neither will you be with Him when He comes in His glory.

If you recoil from the black side of communion, you will not understand its bright, happy period, *"when the Son of man shall come in his glory, and all the holy angels with him."* What, are angels with Him? Yet He does not take up angels; He takes up the seed of Abraham. Are the holy angels with Him? Come, my soul, then you cannot be far from Him. If His friends and His neighbors are called together to see His glory, what do you think will happen if you are married to Him? Will you be distant? Though it will be the Day of Judgment, yet you cannot be far from that heart which, having admitted angels into intimacy, has admitted you into union. Has He not said to you, *"I will even betroth thee unto me in faithfulness: and thou shalt know the LORD"* (Hosea 2:20)? Have not His own lips said, "I am married to you, and My delight is in you"? (See Isaiah 62:4.) If the angels, who are but the friends and the neighbors, will be with Him then, it is abundantly certain that His own beloved Hephzibah, in whom is all His delight, will be near to Him and will be a partaker of His splendor. When He comes in His glory and when His communion with angels is distinctly recognized, then His unity with the church will become apparent.

"Then shall he sit upon the throne of his glory." Here is a repetition of the same reason why it should be your time and mine to receive the reward from Christ if we are found among His faithful servants. When He sits on His throne, it would not be fitting that His own beloved ones should be in the mire. When He was in the place of shame, they were with Him; now that He is on the throne of gold, they must be with Him, too. There would be no oneness—union with Christ would be a mere matter of talk—if it were not certain that, when He is on the throne, they will be on the throne, too.

Further, I want you to notice one particular circumstance regarding the time of the reward. It occurs after He divides the sheep from the goats.

My reward, if I am a child of God, cannot come to me while I am in union with the wicked. Even on earth, you will have the most enjoyment of Christ when you are most separated from this world. Be assured, although the separated path does not seem an easy one and it will certainly entail persecution and the loss of many friends, yet it is the happiest walking in the world. You conforming Christians who can enter into the world's mirth to a certain degree, you cannot know—and never will know as you now are—the inward joys of those who live in lonely but lovely fellowship with Jesus. The nearer you get to the world, the further you must be from Christ. I believe the more thoroughly a bill of divorce is given by your spirit to every earthly object upon which your soul can set itself, the closer will be your communion with your Lord. *"Forget also thine own people, and thy father's house; so shall the king greatly desire thy beauty: for he is thy Lord; and worship thou him"* (Psalm 45:10–11).

It is significant that not until the King separates the sheep from the goats does He say, *"Come, ye blessed."* Though the righteous will have enjoyed a felicity as disembodied spirits, yet even when they are bodily raised from the grave, their felicity will not be fully accomplished until the great Shepherd appears to separate them once and for all by a great gulf, which cannot be passed, from all association with the nations that forget God.

Now then, beloved, these circumstances all put together come to this: the reward for following Christ is not today, is not among the souls of men, is not from men, is not from the excellent of the earth, and is not even bestowed by Jesus while we are here. The glorious crown of life that the Lord's grace will give to His people is reserved for the Second Advent, *"when the* [King] *shall come in his glory, and all his holy angels with him."* Wait with patience, wait with joyful expectation, for He will come. Blessed be the day of His appearing.

THE PORTION OF THE REWARD

We have now to turn to the second point, which concerns the portion of the reward itself. Every word is suggestive. I will not attempt an exhaustive study, but merely to glance at them all.

At His Right Hand

The reward of the righteous is set forth by the loving benediction pronounced to them by the Master, but their very position gives some foreshadowing of it. He put the sheep on His right hand. Heaven is a position of the most elevated dignity authoritatively conferred and of divine satisfaction manifestly enjoyed. God's saints are always at His right hand according to the judgment of faith, but hereafter it will be more clearly manifested. God is pleased to be close to His people and to place them near to Himself in a place of protection.

Sometimes, it seems as if the saints were at His left hand; some of them certainly have less comfort than worldlings. *"I have seen the wicked in great power, and spreading himself like a green bay tree"* (Psalm 37:35). *"Their eyes stand out with fatness: they have more than heart could wish"* (Psalm 73:7). Meanwhile, His people are often made to drink waters of a full cup, and their meat and their drink are bitter with wormwood and gall.

The world is upside down now, but the Gospel has begun to turn it up the right way. However, when the day of grace is over and the day of glory comes, then will it be righted indeed; then those that wandered about in sheepskins and goatskins will be clothed in glittering apparel, being transfigured like the Savior upon Mount Tabor. Then those of whom the world was not worthy will come to a world that will be worthy of them. Then those who were hurried to the stake and to the flames will triumph with chariots of fire and horses of fire, and swell the splendor of the Master's regal appearing.

Yes, beloved, you will eternally be the object of divine satisfaction, not in secret and unmanifested communion, but your state and glory will be revealed before the sons of men. Your persecutors will gnash their teeth when they see you occupying places of honor at His right hand, while they, though far greater than you on earth, are condemned to take the lowest spot. How the rich man will bite his fire-tormented tongue in vain as he sees Lazarus, the beggar on the dunghill, made to sit at the right hand of the King eternal and immortal! Heaven is a place of dignity. "There we will be as the angels," says one, but I believe we will be even more superior than they. Is it not written of Him who in all things is our representative, *"He hath put all things under his feet"* (1 Corinthians 15:27). Even the very seraphs, who are themselves so richly blessed, what are they but *"ministering spirits, sent forth to minister for them who shall be heirs of salvation"* (Hebrews 1:14)?

A Welcome Word

Now, turning to the welcome uttered by the Judge, we find that the first word is *"Come."* It is the symbol of the Gospel. The law said, "Go." The Gospel says, "Come." The Spirit says it in invitation; the bride says it in intercession; believers say it by constantly, laboriously endeavoring to spread abroad the Good News.

Since Jesus says, *"Come,"* we learn that the very essence of heaven is communion. *"Come!"* You came near enough to say, *"Lord, I believe; help thou mine unbelief!"* (Mark 9:24). You looked to Him on the cross and were enlightened. You had fellowship with Him in bearing His cross. You filled up that which was behind of the sufferings of Christ for the sake of His body, which is the church. Still come! Always come! Forever come! Come up from your graves, you risen ones. Come up from among the ungodly, you consecrated ones. Come up from where you cast yourselves down in your humiliation before the Great White Throne. Come up to wear His crown and to sit with Him upon His throne! Oh, that word has heaven lurking within it. It will be to you your joy forever to hear the Savior say to you, *"Come."*

I assert before you that my soul has sometimes been so full of joy I could hold no more when my beloved Lord has said, *"Come,"* to my soul. He has taken me into His banqueting house, His banner of love has waved over my head (Song of Solomon 2:4), and He has taken me away from the world, its cares and its fears, its trials and its joys, up to *"the top of Amana, from the top of Shenir and Hermon"* (Song of Solomon 4:8), where He has manifested Himself to me.

When this *"Come"* will sound in your ear from the Master's lips, there will not be the flesh to drag you back; there will be no sluggishness of spirit, no heaviness of heart. You will come eternally then; you will not mount to descend again, but mount on and on in one blessed *Excelsior* forever and ever. This first word *"Come"* indicates that heaven is a state of communion.

Then it is, *"Come, ye blessed,"* which is a clear declaration that this is a state of happiness. They cannot be more blessed than they are: they have their hearts' desire. Though their hearts have been enlarged and their desires have been expanded by entering into the infinite and getting rid of the cramping influences of corruption and of time, yet even when their desire knows no limitations, they will have all the happiness that the utmost stretch of their souls can by any possibility conceive.

We know this much—and this is all we know —they are supremely blessed. Their blessedness does not come from any secondary joy but from the great primary Source of all good. *"Come, ye blessed of my Father.*" They drink the unadulterated wine at the winepress itself, where it joyously leaps from the bursting clusters. They pluck celestial fruits from the unwithering boughs of the immortal tree. They sit at the fountainhead and drink the waters as they spring with unrivaled freshness from the depths of the heart of Deity. They will not be basking in the beams of the sun, but they will be like Uriel, the angel in the sun. They will dwell in God, and so their souls will be satisfied with favor and will be full, more than full, with His presence and benediction.

Inherit the Kingdom

Now, I would like you to notice that, according to the words used, it is a state where they will recognize their right to be there—a state therefore of perfect freedom, ease, and fearlessness. It says, *"inherit the kingdom."* A man does not fear to lose that which he wins by inheritance from his parent. If heaven had been the subject of earning, we might have feared that our merits had not really deserved it and, therefore, suspected that one day a writ of error would be issued and that we should be ejected. But we do know whose sons we are; we know whose love it is that makes our spirits glad; and when we *"inherit the kingdom,"* we will enter it, not as strangers or as foreigners, but as sons coming to their birthright. Looking over all its streets of gold and surveying all its walls of pearl, we will feel that we are at home in our own house and have an actual right, not through merit but through grace, to everything that is there. It will be a state of heavenly bliss; the Christian will feel that law and justice are on his side and that those stern attributes have brought him there as well as mercy and loving-kindness.

The word *inherit* here connotes full possession and enjoyment. We have inherited in a certain sense before; but now, like heirs who begin to spend their own money and to farm their own acres when they have arrived at full maturity, so will we enter into our heritage. We are not fully grown as yet and, therefore, are not admitted to full possession. But wait awhile; those gray hairs betoken, my beloved, that you are getting ripe. These, my still youthful hair shows me, alas, that I may have to tarry for a little longer. Yet I do not know; the Lord may soon permit me to sleep with my fathers. However, sooner or later as He wills, we will one day come into possession of the land.

Now, if it is sweet to be an heir while you are not of age, what is it to be an heir when you have arrived at mature adulthood? Is it not delightful to sing the hymn and to behold the land of pure delight, whose everlasting spring and never-withering flowers are just across the narrow stream of death? Oh, you sweet fields and you saints immortal who lie down there! When will we be with you and be satisfied? If the mere thinking of heaven ravishes the soul, what must it be to be there, to plunge deep into the stream of blessedness, to dive and find no bottom, to swim and find no shore? To sip of the wine of heaven as we sometimes do makes our hearts so glad that we know not how to express our joy. Oh, what it will be to drink deep and drink again, sitting forever at the table, knowing that the feast will never be over, the cups will never be empty, and there will be no worse wine brought out later, but rather better and better still in infinite progression, if such a thing is possible!

The word *kingdom*, which stands next, indicates the richness of the heritage of saints. It is no petty estate, no alms rooms, no happy corner in obscurity. I heard a good man say he would be content to have a corner behind the door. I will not be. The Lord says we will inherit a kingdom. We should not be satisfied to inherit less, because less than that would not suit our characters. He *"hath made us kings and priests unto God"* (Revelation 1:6), and we must reign forever and ever or be as wretched as deposed monarchs. A king without a kingdom is an unhappy man. If I were a poor servant, an alms room would be a blessing, because it would coincide with my condition and degree. However, if by grace I am made a king, I must have a kingdom, or I will not have attained a position equal to my nature. He who makes us kings will give us a kingdom to fit the natures that He has bestowed on us.

Beloved, more and more strive after that which the Spirit of God will give you, a kingly heart. Do not be among those who are satisfied and contented with the miserable nature of ordinary humanity. The world can be only a child's glass bead to a truly royal spirit; these glittering diadems are only nursery toys to God's kings. The true jewels are up there; the true treasury wealth looks down upon the stars. Do not stint your soul! Get a kingly heart. Ask the King of Kings to give it to you, and beg of Him a royal spirit. Act royally on earth toward your Lord and toward all men, for His sake. Go about the world not as mean men in spirit and act, but as kings and princes of a race superior to the dirt-scrapers who are on their knees crawling in the mud after yellow earth. Then, when your soul is royal, remember with joy that your future inheritance will be all that your kingly soul yearns for in its most royal moments. It will be a state of unutterable richness and wealth of soul.

A Prepared Kingdom

Looking at the word *prepared,* we may conceive this to mean a condition of surpassing excellence. It is a prepared kingdom. It has been prepared for such a long time, and He who prepared it is so wondrously rich in resources that we cannot possibly conceive how excellent it must be. If I might so express an idea, God's common gifts, which He throws away as though they were nothing, are priceless. But what will be the nature of these gifts, upon which the infinite mind of God has been set for ages and ages in order that they may reach the highest degree of excellence?

Long before Christmas chimes were ringing, a mother was so glad to think that her boy was coming home after his first quarter away at school that she began preparing and planning all sorts of joys for him. Well might his holidays be happy when his mother had been contriving to make them so. In an infinitely nobler manner, the great God has prepared a kingdom for His people; He has thought, "That will please them, and that will bless them, and this will make them superlatively happy." He has prepared the kingdom to perfection.

If that were not enough, as the glorious man Christ Jesus went up from earth to heaven, you know what He said when He departed: *"I go to prepare a place for you"* (John 14:2). We know that the infinite God can prepare a place fitting for a finite creature, but the words smile so sweetly at us as we read that Jesus Himself, who is a man and therefore knows our hearts' desires, has had a finger in it; He has prepared it, too. It is a kingdom prepared for you, upon which the thoughts of God have been set to make it excellent *"from the foundation of the world."*

Chosen Inheritors

We must not pause. This is a *"kingdom prepared for you."* Mark that! I must confess that I do not like certain expressions I hear sometimes which imply that heaven is prepared for some who will never reach it, prepared for those who will be driven as accursed ones into the place of torment. I know there is a sacred verse which says, "[Let] *no man take thy crown*" (Revelation 3:11), but that refers to the crown of ministerial success rather than of eternal glory. An expression that grated on my ears, from the lips of a certain good man, went something like this: "There is a heaven prepared for all of you; but if you are not faithful, you will not win it. There is a crown in heaven laid up for you; but if you are not faithful, it will be without a wearer." I do not believe it; I cannot believe it. That any crown of eternal life which is laid up for the *"blessed of* [the] *Father"* would ever be given to anybody else or left without a possessor, I do not believe. I dare not conceive of crowns in heaven with nobody to wear them.

Do you think that in heaven, when the whole number of saints is complete, you will find a number of unused crowns? "Ah, who are these crowns for? Where are the heads for these?" "They are in hell!" Then, brother, I have no particular desire to be in heaven. If all of the family of Christ are not there, my soul will be wretched and forlorn because of their sad loss, for I am in union with them all. If one soul that believed in Jesus does not get there, I would lose respect for the promise and respect for the Master, too. He must keep His word to every soul that rests in Him.

If your God has actually prepared a place for His people, made provision for them, and then been disappointed, He is no God to me. I could not adore a disappointed God. I do not believe in such a God. Such a being would not be God at all. The notion of disappointment in His eternal preparations is not consistent with Deity. Talk thus of Jupiter and Venus if you please, but the infinite Jehovah is dishonored by being mentioned in such a connection. He has prepared a place for you.

Here is personal election. He has made a distinct ordinance for every one of His people so that where He is, there they will be also (John 14:3).

Time of the Preparation

"Prepared...from the foundation of the world." Here is eternal election appearing before men were created, preparing a crown before heads were made to wear it. Thus, before the starry skies began to gleam, God had carried out the decree of election in a measure that will be perfected, when Christ comes again, to the praise of the glory of His grace, *"who worketh all things after the counsel of his own will"* (Ephesians 1:11). Our portion then is one that has been prepared from all eternity for us according to the election of God's grace, one suitable to the loftiest character to which we can ever attain, that will consist in nearness to Christ, communion with God, and standing forever in a place of dignity and happiness.

THE RIGHTEOUS INHERITORS

Finally, we want to consider carefully the people who will inherit the kingdom. These righteous inheritors are recognizable by a secret and by a public character. Their name is *"blessed of [the] Father."* The Father chose them, gave His Son for them, justified them through Christ, preserved them in Christ Jesus, adopted them into the family, and now has accepted them into His own house.

Their nature is described in the word *inherit*. Since none can inherit but sons, they have been born again and have received the nature of God. Having escaped the corruption that is in the world through lust, they have become partakers of the divine nature and are thus sons. Their appointment is mentioned: *"Inherit the kingdom prepared for you, from before the foundation of the world."* Their name is *"blessed"*; their nature is that of a child; their appointment is that by God's decree.

Behavior of the Righteous

We want to look the actions of the inheritors, their outward behavior, at for a moment. They appear to have been distinguished among men for deeds of charity, and these were not in any way associated with ceremonies or outward observances. It is not said that they preached—they did so, some of them. It is not said that they prayed—they must have done so, or they would not have been spiritually alive. The actions that are selected as typical are actions of charity to the indigent and forlorn.

Why focus on charitable acts? I think so that the general audience assembled around the throne would know how to appreciate this evidence of their newborn nature. The King might think more of their prayers than of their alms, but the multitude would not. He speaks so as to gain the verdict of all assembled. Even their enemies could not object to His calling those blessed who had performed these actions.

If there is any action that wins for men the universal consent to their goodness, it is an action by which men would be served. *"Against such there is no law"* (Galatians 5:23). I have never heard of any state in which there was a law against clothing the naked and feeding the hungry. Humanity, even when its conscience is so seared that it cannot see its own sinfulness, can still detect the virtuousness of feeding the poor. Undoubtedly, this is one reason why these actions were selected.

Evidences of Grace

Moreover, they may have been chosen as evidences of grace because, as actions, they are a wonderful means of separating between the hypocrite and the true Christian. Dr. Gill has an idea—and perhaps he was right—that this is not a picture of the general judgment but of the judgment of the professing church. If so, it is all the more reasonable to conclude that these works of mercy are selected as appropriately discerning between the hypocrite and the sincere. I fear that there are some of you who loudly profess your faith who could not stand the test. "Good, praying people," they call you, but what do you give to the Lord? Your religion has not touched your pockets.

This does not apply to some of you, for there are many of whom I would venture to speak before the bar of God, that I know your substance to be consecrated to the Lord and His poor, and I have sometimes thought that beyond your means you have given both to the poor and to God's cause. However, there are others of a very different disposition. Now, I will give you in plain English a lesson that none can fail to understand. You may talk about your religion until you have worn your tongue out, and you may get others to believe you; you may remain in the church twenty years, and nobody ever detect in you or even suspect you of anything like an inconsistency; but, if it is in your power and you do nothing to relieve the necessities of the poor members of Christ's body, you will be damned as surely as if you were drunkards or whoremongers. If you have no care for God's church, this text applies to you, and will as surely sink you to the lowest hell as if you had been common blasphemers. That is very plain English, but it is the plain meaning of my text, and it is at my peril that I flinch from telling you of it.

"I was an hungered, and ye gave me"—what? Good advice, yes, but no meat. "I was thirsty, and ye gave me"—what? A tract, and no drink. "I was naked, and ye"—gave me what? Your good wishes, but no clothes. "I was a stranger and ye"—what? You pitied me, but you did not take me in. "I was sick, and ye"—what? You said you could recommend a doctor for me, but you did not visit me. "I was in prison"—God's servant, a persecuted one, put in prison for Christ's sake—and you said I should be more cautious, but you did not stand by my side and take a share of the blame and bear with me reproach for the truth's sake. You see, this is a very terrible winnowing fan to some of you begrudging ones whose main object in life is to get all you can and hold it fast, but it is a fan that frequently must be used. Whoever tries to spare you, by the grace of God, I will not; but I will labor to be ever more bold in denouncing sin.

"Well," says one, "what is all of that to those who are so poor that they have nothing to give away?" My dearly beloved, do you notice how beautifully the text takes care of you? It hints that there are some who cannot give bread to the hungry and clothes to the naked, but what about them? They are the people spoken of as *"the least of these my brethren"* (Matthew 25:40), who receive the blessing of kindness. This passage comforts the poor and by no means condemns them.

Certain of us honestly give to the poor all we can spare, and then, of course, everybody comes to such a person. When we then say, "Really, I cannot give any more," somebody snarls and says, "Do you call yourself a Christian?" "Yes, I do. I should not call myself a Christian if I gave away other people's money; I should not call myself a Christian if I gave away what I do not have; I should call myself a thief, pretending to be charitable when I could not pay my debts." I have a very great pity indeed for those people who get into the bankruptcy court: I do not mean I pity the debtors, for I have seldom much sympathy with them; I have a good deal of feeling for the creditors who lose by having trusted dishonest people.

If any man thinks that he would live beyond his means in order to get a charitable character, my dear brother, you are wrong. That action is in itself wrong. What you have to give must be that which is your own. "But I would have to tighten my way of living," says one, "if I did it." Well, pinch yourself! I do not think there is half the pleasure in doing good until you get to the pinching point. This remark, of course, applies only to those of us of moderate means, who can soon distribute our alms and get down to the pinching point where we begin to feel, "Now, I must do without that; now I must curtail this thing in order to do more good." Oh, you cannot know! It is then when you really can feel, "Now, I have not given God merely the cheese parings and candle ends that I could not use, but I have really cut out for my Master a good piece of the loaf; I have not given Him the old crusts that were getting moldy, but I have given Him a piece of my own daily bread; and I am glad to do it, if I can show my love to Jesus Christ by denying myself."

If you are doing this—if you are thus, out of love to Jesus, feeding the hungry and clothing the naked—I believe that these actions are given as examples because they are such blessed detectives between the hypocrites and the really godly people. When you read *"for"* in this passage, you must not understand that their reward is because of this, but that they have proved to be God's servants by this. So, while they do not merit it because of these actions, yet these actions show that they were saved by grace, which is evidenced by the fact that Christ has wrought such works in them. If Christ does not work such things in you, you have no part in Him; if you have not produced such works as these, you have not believed in Jesus.

Now, somebody says, "Then I intend to give to the poor in the future in order that I may have this reward." Ah, but you are very much mistaken if you do that.

The Duke of Burgundy was waited upon by a poor man, a very loyal subject, who brought him a very large root that he had grown. He was a very poor man indeed, and every root he grew in his garden was of consequence to him. But, merely as a loyal offering, he brought to his prince the largest his little garden produced. The prince was so pleased with the man's evident loyalty and affection that he gave him a very large sum. Seeing this, the duke's steward thought, "Well, I see this pays; this man got fifty pounds for his large root. I think I will make the duke a present." So, he bought a horse, and he reckoned that he should have in return ten times as much for it as it was worth. He presented it to the duke with that view in mind. The duke, like a wise man, quietly accepted the horse and gave the greedy steward nothing. That was all.

Likewise, you say, "Well, here is a Christian man, and he gets rewarded; he has been giving to the poor, helping the Lord's church, and he is saved; the thing pays, so I will make a little investment, too." But, you see, the steward did not give the horse out of any idea of loyalty and kindness and love to the duke, but out of very great love of himself, and therefore had no return. If you perform deeds of charity with the idea of getting to heaven by them, it is yourself that you are feeding and yourself that you are clothing. All your virtue is not virtue—it is rank selfishness; it smells strongly of selfhood, and Christ will never accept it. You will never hear Him say "thank you" for it. You served yourself, and no reward is due.

You must first come to the Lord Jesus Christ and look to Him to save you. You must forever renounce all ideas of doing anything to save yourself. But once, having been saved, you will be able to give to the poor and needy without selfishness mixing with your motives, and you will get a reward of grace for the love-token that you have given.

It is necessary to believe in Christ in order to be capable of true virtue of the highest order. It is necessary to trust Jesus and to be fully saved yourself before there is any value in your feeding the hungry or clothing the naked.

May God give you grace to go to my wounded Master and to rest in the precious atonement which He has made for human sin. When you have done that, being loved so greatly, may you show that you love in return; being purchased so dearly, may you live for Him that bought you. Among the actions by which you prove it, let these gleam and glisten like God-given jewels: the visiting of the sick, the comforting of the needy, the relieving of the distressed, and the helping of the weak. May God accept these offerings as they come from gracious souls. To Him be praise evermore. Amen.

Chapter Three

The Ascension and the Second Advent Practically Considered

And while they looked steadfastly toward heaven
as he went up, behold, two men stood
by them in white apparel;
Which also said, Ye men of Galilee, why stand ye
gazing up into heaven? this same Jesus, which is
taken up from you into heaven, shall so come in like
manner as ye have seen him go into heaven.
—Acts 1:10–11

Four great events shine out brightly in our Savior's story. All Christian minds delight to dwell upon His birth, His death, His Resurrection, and His Ascension. These make four rungs in that ladder of light, the foot of which is upon the earth, and the top of which reaches to heaven. We could not afford to dispense with any one of those four events, nor would it be profitable for us to forget or to underestimate the value of any one of them.

That the Son of God was born of a woman creates in us the intense delight of a brotherhood springing out of a common humanity. That Jesus once suffered unto the death for our sins, and thereby made a full atonement for us, is the rest and life of our spirits. The manger and the cross together are divine seals of love. That the Lord Jesus rose again from the dead is the guarantee of our justification, as well as a transcendently delightful assurance of the resurrection of all His people and of their eternal life in Him. Has He not said, *"Because I live, ye shall live also"* (John 14:19)? The Resurrection of Christ is the morning star of our future glory. Equally delightful is the remembrance of His Ascension. No song is sweeter than this: *"Thou hast ascended on high, thou hast led captivity captive: thou hast received gifts for men; yea, for the rebellious also, that the LORD God might dwell among them"* (Psalm 68:18).

Each one of those four events points to a future event, and they all lead up to it: the fifth link in the golden chain is our Lord's second and most glorious Advent. Nothing is mentioned between His ascent and His decent. True, a rich history comes between, but it lies in a valley between two stupendous mountains. We step from alp to alp as we journey in meditation from the Ascension to the Second Advent. I say that each of the previous four events points to it. Had He not come a first time in humiliation, born under the law, He could not *"appear the second time without sin unto salvation"* (Hebrews 9:28) in amazing glory.

Because He died once, we rejoice *"that Christ being raised from the dead dieth no more; death hath no more dominion over him"* (Romans 6:9). Therefore, He comes to destroy that last enemy

(1 Corinthians 15:26), which He has already conquered through His death (Hebrews 2:14). It is our joy, as we think of our Redeemer as risen, to feel that, in consequence of His rising, the trump of the archangel will assuredly sound for the awaking of all His slumbering people, when *"the Lord himself shall descend from heaven with a shout"* (1 Thessalonians 4:16). As for His Ascension, He could not descend a second time if He had not first ascended. But, having perfumed heaven with His presence and prepared a place for His people, we may aptly expect that He will come again and receive us unto Himself, that where He is, there we may be also (John 14:3). I want you, therefore, as you pass with joyful footsteps over these four grand events, as your faith leaps from His birth to His death, from His Resurrection to His Ascension, to be looking forward and hastening unto this crowning fact of our Lord's history: before long, He will come in like manner as He was seen going up into heaven (Acts 1:11).

A CLARIFYING DEPICTION

At this present moment, we will start from the Ascension. If I had sufficient imagination, I would like to picture our Lord and the eleven walking up the side of Olivet, communing as they went, a happy company with a solemn awe upon them but with an intense joy in having fellowship with each other. Each disciple was glad to think that his dear Lord and Master, who had been crucified, was now among them, not only alive, but also surrounded with a mysterious safety and glory that none could disturb. The enemy was as still as a stone. No dog moved his tongue; his bitterest foes made no sign during the days of our Lord's afterlife below.

The company moved onward peacefully towards Bethany, which they all knew and loved. The Savior seemed drawn there at the time of His Ascension, even as men's minds return to old and well-loved scenes when they are about to depart this world. His happiest moments on earth had been spent beneath the roof where Mary and Martha and their brother Lazarus lived. Perhaps it was best for the disciples that He should leave them at that place where He had been most hospitably entertained, to show that He departed in peace and not in anger. There they had seen Lazarus raised from the dead by Him who was now to be taken up from them: the memory of the triumphant past would help the tried faith of the present. There they had heard the voice saying, *"Loose him, and let him go"* (John 11:44); there they might aptly see their Lord loosed from all bonds of earthly gravitation that He might go to His Father and their Father. The memories of the place might help to calm their minds and arouse their spirits to that fullness of joy which ought to attend the glorifying of their Lord.

But they had come to a standstill, having reached the crest of the hill. The Savior stood conspicuously in the center of the group. Following a most instructive discourse, He pronounced a blessing upon them as He lifted His pierced hands.

While He was lifting them and was pronouncing words of love, He began to rise from the earth. To their astonishment, He had risen above them all! In a moment He had passed beyond the olives, which, with their silvery sheen, seemed to be lit up by His milder radiance. While the disciples were looking, the Lord had ascended into midair, and speedily He had risen to the regions of the clouds. They stood, spellbound with astonishment, as suddenly a bright cloud, like a chariot of God, bore Him away. That cloud concealed Him from mortal gaze. *"Though we have known Christ after the flesh, yet now henceforth know we him no more"* (2 Corinthians 5:16). They were riveted to the spot, and very naturally so. They lingered for a long time in that place. They stood with streaming eyes, awestruck, still looking upward.

It was not the Lord's will that they should remain inactive for long; their reverie was interrupted. They might have stood there until wonder saddened into fear. As it was, they remained long enough, for the angel's words may be accurately translated, "Why have you stood, gazing up into heaven?"

Their lengthened gaze needed to be interrupted. Therefore, two shining ones, such as before met the women at the sepulcher, were sent to them. These messengers of God appeared in human form so that they might not alarm them, and in white raiment as if to remind them that all was bright and joyous. These white-robed ministers stood with the disciples as if they would willingly join their company. Since none of the eleven would break the silence, the men in white raiment began the discourse. Addressing them in the usual celestial style, they asked a question that contained its own answer and then went on to tell their message. As they had once said to the women, *"Why seek ye the living among the dead? He is not here, but is risen"* (Luke 24:5–6), so did they now say, *"Ye men of Galilee, why stand ye gazing up into heaven? this same Jesus, which is taken up from you into heaven, shall so come in like manner as ye have seen him go into heaven."* The angels showed their knowledge of them by calling them, *"men of Galilee,"* and reminded them that they were yet upon earth by recalling their place of birth.

Brought back to their senses, their reverie over, the apostles at once girded up their loins for active service. They did not need to be told twice but hastened to Jerusalem. The vision of angels had singularly brought them back into the world of actual life again, so that they obeyed Christ's command, *"Tarry ye in the city of Jerusalem"* (Luke 24:49). They seemed to say, "The taking up of our Master is not a thing to weep about. He has gone to His throne and to His glory, and He said it was expedient for us that He should go away. He will now send us the promise of the Father; we scarcely know what it will be like, but let us, in obedience to His will, make our way to the place where He charged us to await the gift of power."

Do you not see them going down the side of Olivet, taking that Sabbath-day journey into the cruel and wicked city without a thought of fear, having no dread of the bloodthirsty crew who slew their Lord, but happily remembering their Lord's exaltation and in the expectation of a wonderful display of His power? They held fellowship of the most delightful kind with one another. Shortly, they entered into the Upper Room where, in protracted prayer and communion, they waited for the promise of the Father.

I fear I have no imagination; I have barely mentioned the incidents in the simplest language. Yet, try to realize the scene because it will be helpful to do so since our Lord Jesus is to *"come in like manner"* as the disciples saw Him ascend.

My first topic for discussion will be the gentle chiding administered by the shining ones: *"Ye men of Galilee, why stand ye gazing up into heaven?"* Secondly, I will consider the cheering description of our Lord that the white-robed messengers used: *"This same Jesus."* Finally, I wish to examine the practical truth which they taught: *"This same Jesus, which is taken up from you into heaven, shall so come in like manner as ye have seen him go into heaven."*

A Gentle Chiding

First, then, is a gentle chiding. It was not sharply uttered by men dressed in black who used harsh speech to upbraid the servants of God severely for what was rather a mistake than a fault. No, the language is strengthening, yet tender; the form of a question allows them to reprove themselves rather than to be reproved; and the tone is that of brotherly love and affectionate concern.

Doing What Seems Right

Notice that what these saintly men were doing seems at first sight to be very right. I think, if Jesus were among us now, we would fix our eyes upon Him and never withdraw them. He is altogether lovely, and it would seem wicked to yield our eyesight to any inferior object as long as He was able to be seen. When He ascended up into heaven, it was the duty of His friends to look upon Him. It can never be wrong to look up; we are often directed to do so. It is even a holy saying of the psalmist: *"I* [will] *direct my prayer unto thee, and will look up"* (Psalm 5:3), and, *"I will lift up mine eyes unto the hills, from whence cometh my help"* (Psalm 121:1). If it is right to look up into heaven, it must be still more right to look up while Jesus rises to the place of His glory. Surely it would have been wrong if they had looked anywhere else.

It was due to the Lamb of God that they beheld Him as long as eyes could follow Him. He is the Sun; where should eyes be turned but to His light? He is the King; where should courtiers within the palace gate turn their eyes but to their King as He ascends to His throne? The truth is that there was nothing wrong in their looking up into heaven.

However, they went a little farther than looking—they stood *"gazing."* A little excess in right action may be faulty. It may be wise to look but foolish to gaze. There is a very thin line sometimes between that which is commendable and that which is censurable. There is a golden mean that is not easy to keep. The exact path of right is often as narrow as a razor's edge, and he who does not err either on the right hand or on the left must be wise.

Look is ever the right word. After all, it is *"Look unto me, and be ye saved"* (Isaiah 45:22). Look, yes, look steadfastly and intently. Your posture should always be that of one *"looking unto Jesus"* (Hebrews 12:2) throughout life.

However, there is a gazing which is not commendable, when the look becomes not that of reverent worship, but of an presumptuous curiosity; when there mingles with the desire to know what should be known, a prying into that which it is for God's glory to conceal. Beloved, it is of little use to look up into an empty heaven. If Christ Himself is not visible in heaven, then in vain do we gaze, since there is nothing for a saintly eye to see. When the person of Jesus was gone out of the azure vault above them and the cloud had effectively concealed Him, why should they continue to gaze when God Himself had drawn the curtain? If infinite wisdom had withdrawn the object upon which they desired to gaze, what would their gazing be but a sort of reflection upon the wisdom that had removed their Lord?

Yet, it did seem very right. Thus, certain things that you and I may do may appear right, yet we may need to be chided out of them into something better. They may be right in themselves, but they are not appropriate for the occasion, not seasonable, nor expedient. They may be right up to a point, and then they may touch the boundary of excess. A steadfast gaze into heaven may be to a devout soul a high order of worship, but if this fills up much of the working time, it might become the most idle form of folly.

Doing What Comes Naturally

However, I cannot help adding that it was very natural. I do not wonder that the whole eleven stood gazing up, for if I had been there, I am sure I should have done the same. How struck they must have been with the ascent of the Master out of their midst! You would be amazed if someone from among your own number now began to ascend into heaven, would you not? Our Lord did not gradually melt away from sight as a phantom or dissolve into thin air as a mere apparition. The Savior did not disappear in that way at all. He rose, and they saw that it was His very self that was so rising. His own body, the material in which He had veiled Himself, actually, distinctly, and literally rose to heaven before their eyes. I repeat, the Lord did not dissolve and disappear like a vision of the night, but He evidently rose until the clouds intervened and they could see Him no more.

I think I should have stood looking at the very place where His cloudy chariot had been. I know it would be idle to continue so to do, but our hearts often urge us on to acts that we could not justify logically. Hearts are not to be argued with. Sometimes you stand by a grave where one is buried whom you dearly loved. You go there often to weep; you cannot help it. The place is precious to you. Yet you could not prove that you do any good by your visits. Perhaps you even injure yourself thereby and deserve to be gently chided with the question, Why?

It may be the most natural thing in the world, and yet it may not be a wise thing to do. The Lord allows us to do that which is innocently natural, but He will not have us carry it too far because then it might foster an evil nature. Hence, He sends an interrupting messenger—not an angel with a sword, or even a rod—but He sends some man in white raiment. I mean one who is both cheerful and holy, and who, by his conduct or his words, suggests to us the question, *"Why stand ye gazing?" Cui bono?* What will be the benefit? What will it avail? Thus, our understanding being called into action, and we, being men of thought, answer within ourselves, "This will not do. We must not stand gazing here forever." Therefore, we arouse ourselves to get back to the Jerusalem of practical life, where we hope to do service for our Master in the power of God.

Notice, then, that the disciples were doing that which seemed to be right and what was evidently very natural. But, note also that it is very easy to carry the apparently right and the absolutely natural too far. Let us take heed to ourselves and often ask our hearts, Why?

Acting without Reason

Next, notice that what they did was not justifiable, based upon strict reason. While Christ was going up, it was proper that they should adoringly look at Him. He might almost have said, "If you see Me when I am taken up, a double portion of My spirit shall rest upon you." (See 2 Kings 2:9–10.) They did well to look where He led the way. However, when He was gone, to remain gazing was an act that they could not exactly explain to themselves and could not justify to others. Try asking the question like this: "What purpose will be fulfilled by your continuing to gaze into the sky? He is gone; it is absolutely certain that He is gone. He is taken up, and God Himself has manifestly concealed all trace of Him by bidding yonder cloud to sail in between Him and you. Why gaze you still? He told you, *'I go unto my Father'* (John 14:12). Why stand and gaze?"

We may, under the influence of great love, act unwisely. I well remember seeing the action of a woman whose only son was emigrating to a distant colony. I stood in the station, noticing her many tears and her frequent embraces of her boy; but the train came, and he entered the carriage. After the train had pulled out from the station, she was foolish enough to break away from friends who sought to detain her. She ran along the platform, leaped down on the railroad tracks, and pursued the flying train. It was natural, but it would have been better left undone. What was the use of it?

We should abstain from acts which serve no practical purpose, for in this life we have neither time nor strength to waste in fruitless action. The disciples would be wise to cease gazing, for nobody would be benefited by it, and they would not themselves be blessed. What is the use of gazing when there is nothing to see? Well did the angels ask, *"Why stand ye gazing up into heaven?"*

Again, ask another question: What precept were they obeying when they stood gazing up into heaven? If you have a command from God to do a certain thing, you need not inquire into the reason of the command; it is disobedient to question God's will. However, when there is no precept whatever, why persevere in an act that evidently does not promise to bring any blessing? Who had ordered them to stand gazing up into heaven? If Christ had done so, then in Christ's name let them stand like statues and never turn their heads. But, as He had not bidden them, why did they do what He had not directed and leave undone what He had commanded? He had strictly charged them that they should tarry at Jerusalem until they were *"endued with power from on high"* (Luke 24:49). Thus, what they did was not justifiable.

Acting Unproductively

Here is the practical point for us: What they did, we are very apt to imitate. "Oh," you say, "I would never stand gazing up into heaven." I am not sure of that. Some Christians are very curious but not obedient. Plain precepts are neglected, but they seek to solve difficult problems. I remember a person who always was dwelling on the vials and seals and trumpets; he was great at apocalyptic symbols. But he had seven children, and he had no family prayer. If he had left the vials and trumpets and tended to his boys' and girls' upbringing, it would have been far better.

I have known men marvelously learned in Daniel and specially instructed in Ezekiel, but singularly forgetful of the twentieth chapter of Exodus and not very clear about the eighth chapter of Romans. I do not speak with any blame of such folks for studying Daniel and Ezekiel—quite the opposite. Yet I wish they had been more zealous for the conversion of the sinners in their homes and neighborhoods and more careful to assist the poor saints. I admit the value of the study of the feet of the image in Nebachadnezzar's vision and the importance of knowing the kingdoms that make up the ten toes, but I do not see the propriety of allowing such studies to override the commonplace activities of practical godliness. If the time spent over obscure theological propositions were given to a mission in the dim alley near the man's house, more benefit would come to man and more glory to God.

Do not misunderstand, beloved. I would have you understand all mysteries, if you could. But do not forget that our chief business here below is to cry, *"Behold the Lamb!"* (John 1:29). By all means, read and search until you know all that the Lord has revealed concerning things to come, but first of all see to it that your children are brought to the Savior's feet and that you are workers together with God in the building of His church. The dense mass of misery and ignorance and sin that is round about us on every side demands all our powers. If you do not respond to the call, though I am not a man in white apparel, I venture to say to you, "You men of Christendom, why do you stand gazing up into the mysteries when so much is to be done for Jesus and you are leaving it undone?" Oh, you who are curious but not obedient, I fear I address you in vain, but I have done so nevertheless. May the Holy Spirit apply this to your hearts.

Others are contemplative but not active; they are much given to the study of Scripture and to meditation but not *"zealous of good works"* (Titus 2:14). Contemplation is so scarce these days that I could wish there were a thousand times as much of it. However, in the case to which I refer, everything runs in the one channel of thought: all time is spent in reading, in enjoyment, in rapture, and in pious leisure.

Religion never ought to become the subject of selfishness, yet I fear some treat it as if its chief end were personal spiritual gratification. When a man's religion totally lies in his saving only himself and in enjoying holy things for himself, there is a disease upon him. When his judgment of a sermon is based upon the one question, "Did it feed me?" it is a swinish judgment. There is such a thing as getting a swinish religion in which you are yourself first, yourself second, yourself third, yourself to the utmost end. Did Jesus ever think or speak in that fashion? Contemplation of Christ Himself may be so carried out as to lead you away from Him. The recluse meditates on Jesus, but he is as unlike the busy, self-denying Jesus as any can be. Meditation, unattended by active service in the spreading of the Gospel among men, well deserves the rebuke of the angel, *"Ye men of Galilee, why stand ye gazing up into heaven?"*

Acting Impatiently

Moreover, some are careful and anxious and deliriously impatient for some supernatural intervention. We get at times into a sad state of mind because we do not see the kingdom of Christ advancing as we desire. I suppose it is with you as it is with me: I begin to fret and am deeply troubled. I feel that there is good reason I should be upset, because *"truth is fallen in the streets"* (Isaiah 59:14) and the *"day of trouble, and of rebuke, and of blasphemy"* (Isaiah 37:3) is upon us. Then, I pine because the Master is away, and I cry, "When will He be back again? Oh, why are His chariots so long in coming? Why does He tarry through the ages?" Then, if you are like me, our desires sour into impatience, and we commence gazing up into heaven, looking for His coming with a restlessness that does not allow us to discharge our duties as we should. Whenever anybody gets into that state, this is the word: *"Ye men of Galilee, why stand ye gazing up into heaven?"*

Acting from Wrong Desires

In certain cases this uneasiness has drawn to itself a wrong expectation of immediate wonders and an intense desire for sign-seeing. Ah, me, what fanaticism comes of this! In America years ago, a man came forward who declared that on a certain day the Lord would come. This man led a great company to believe his crazy predictions. Many took their horses and fodder for two or three days and went out into the woods, expecting to be all the more likely to see all that was to be seen when once away from the crowded city. All over the States, there were people who had made ascension dresses in which to soar into the air in proper costume. They waited, and they waited, and I am sure that no text could have been more appropriate for them than this: *"Ye men of* [America], *why stand ye gazing up into heaven?"* Nothing came of it, yet there are thousands in England and America who only need a fanatical leader for them to run into similar folly.

The desire to know the times and seasons is a craze with many poor bodies whose insanity runs in that particular groove. All natural occurrences are *"signs of the times"* (Matthew 16:3)—signs, I may add, which they do not understand. Earthquakes are special favorites with them. "Now," they cry, "the Lord is coming," as if there had not been earthquakes of the sort we have heard of lately hundreds of times since our Lord went up into heaven. When the prophetic earthquakes occur in diverse places, we will know of it without the warnings of these brothers. What a number of people have been infatuated by the number of the beast and have been ready to leap for joy because they have found the number 666 in some famous person's name. Why, everybody's name will yield that number if you treat it judiciously and use the numerals of Greece, or Rome, or Egypt, or China, or Timbuktu. I feel weary with the silly way in which some people make toys out of Scripture and play with texts as with a pack of cards.

Whenever you meet with a man who promotes himself as a prophet, keep out of his way in the future. When you hear of signs and wonders, turn to your Lord, and *"in your patience possess ye your souls"* (Luke 21:19). *"The just shall live by* [his] *faith"* (Romans 1:17). There is no other way of living among wild enthusiasts.

Believe in God, and ask not for miracles and marvels or the knowledge of times and seasons. To know when the Lord will restore the kingdom is not in your scope. Remember this verse: *"It is not for you to know the times or the seasons"* (Acts 1:7). If I were introduced into a room where a large number of parcels were stored and told that there was something good for me, I would begin to look for anything with my name on it. If I came upon a parcel and saw in big letters, *"It is not for you,"* I would leave it alone. Here, then, is a package of knowledge marked, *"It is not for you to know the times or the seasons, which the Father hath put in his own power"* (Acts 1:7). Cease to meddle with matters that are concealed, and be satisfied to know the things that are clearly revealed.

A Cheering Description

Next, I want you to notice the cheering description which these bright spirits gave concerning our Lord. They described Him as *"this same Jesus."* I appreciate the description all the more because it came from those who knew Him: He was *"seen of angels"* (1 Timothy 3:16). They had watched Him all His life long, and they knew Him. When they, having just seen Him rise to His Father and His God, said of Him, *"This same Jesus,"* then I know by an infallible testimony that He was the same, and that He is the same.

Jesus Is Alive

Jesus is gone, but He still exists. He has left us, but He is not dead. He has not dissolved into nothing like the mist of the morning. *"This same Jesus"* is gone up unto His Father's throne, and He is there today as certainly as He once stood at Pilate's bar. As surely as He did hang upon the cross, so surely does He, the selfsame man, sit upon the throne of God and reign over creation.

I like to compare the positive identity of the Christ in the seventh heaven with the Christ in the lowest depths of agony. The Christ they spat upon is now the Christ whose name the cherubim and seraphim are singing day without night. The Christ they scourged is He before whom principalities and powers delight to cast their crowns. Think of it, and be glad. Do not stand gazing up into heaven after a myth or a dream. Jesus lives; mind that you live also. Do not loiter as if you had nothing at all to do or as if the kingdom of God had come to an end because Jesus is gone from the earth as to His bodily presence. It is not all over; He still lives, and He has given you work to do until He comes. Therefore, go and do it.

"This same Jesus." I love that word *Jesus*, because it means a Savior. Oh, you anxious sinners, the name of Him who has gone up into His glory is full of invitation to you! Will you not come to *"this same Jesus"*? This is He who opened the eyes of the blind and brought forth the prisoners out of incarceration. He is doing the same thing today. Oh, that your eyes may see His light! He who touched the lepers and raised the dead is the same Jesus still, *"able also to save them to the uttermost that come unto God by him"* (Hebrews 7:25). Oh, that you may look and live! You have only to come to Him by faith, as she did who touched the hem of His garment. You have but to cry to Him as the blind man did whose sight He restored, for He is the same Jesus, bearing about with Him the same tender love for guilty men and the same readiness to receive and cleanse all that come to Him by faith.

The Same Jesus Will Return

"This same Jesus." Why, that must have meant that He who is in heaven is the same Christ who was on earth, but it must also mean that He who is to come will be the same Jesus that went up into heaven. There is no change in our blessed Master's nature, nor will there ever be. There is a great change in His condition:

> The Lord shall come, but not the same
> As once in lowliness He came,
> A humble man before His foes,
> A weary man, and full of woes.

He will be *"this same Jesus"* in nature though not in condition: He will possess the same tenderness when He comes to judge, the same gentleness of heart when all the glories of heaven and earth encircle His brow. Our eyes will see Him in that day, and we will recognize Him, not only by the nail-prints, but by the very look of His countenance, by the character that gleams from that marvelous face. We will say, "It is Jesus! 'Tis He! The same Christ that went up from the top of Olivet from the midst of His disciples!" Go to Him with your troubles as you would have done when He was here. Look forward to His Second Coming without dread. Look for Him with that joyous expectancy with which you would welcome Jesus of Bethany, who loved Mary, Martha, and Lazarus.

Preceding that sweet title came this question: *"Why stand ye gazing up into heaven?"* They might have said, "We stay here because we do not know where to go. Our Master is gone." But, oh, it is the same Jesus, and He is coming again; so go down to Jerusalem and get to work directly. Do not worry yourselves. No grave accident has occurred. It is not a disaster that Christ has gone, but an advance in His work. Despisers tell us nowadays, "Your cause is done, for Christianity has become obsolete! Your divine Christ is gone; we have not seen a trace of His miracle-working hand, nor heard a whisper of that voice which no man could rival." Our response should be that we are not standing, gazing into heaven; we are not paralyzed because Jesus is away. He lives; our great Redeemer lives. Although it is our delight to lift up our eyes because we expect His coming, it is equally our delight to turn our heavenly gazing into an earthward watching and to go down into the city, there to tell that Jesus is risen, that men are to be saved by faith in Him, and that *"whosoever believeth in him should not perish, but have everlasting life"* (John 3:16).

We are not defeated—far from it. His Ascension is not a retreat, but an advance. His tarrying is not for lack of power, but because of the abundance of His long-suffering. The victory is not questionable. All things work for it: all the hosts of God are mustering for the final charge. This same Jesus is mounting His white horse to lead forth the armies of heaven, conquering and to conquer.

A GREAT PRACTICAL TRUTH

My third point concerns the great practical truth found in the text. This truth is not one that is to keep us gazing into heaven, but one that is to make each of us go to his own house to render earnest service. What is this truth?

Jesus Is in Heaven

First, this truth is that Jesus is gone into heaven. Jesus is gone! Jesus is gone! It sounds like a bell ringing. Jesus is taken up from you into heaven—that sounds like marriage chimes. He is gone, but He is gone up to the hills from where He can survey the battle—up to the throne from which He can send us help. The reserve forces of the Omnipotent stood waiting until their Captain came; now that He has come into the center of the universe, He can send legions of angels or raise up hosts of men for the help of His cause.

I see every reason for going out into the world and getting to work because He is ascended into heaven. Moreover, *"all power is given unto* [Him] *in heaven and in earth"* (Matthew 28:18). Is not this a good argument to spur you on: *"Go ye therefore, and teach all nations, baptizing them in the name of the Father, and of the Son, and of the Holy Ghost"* (Matthew 28:19)?

Jesus Will Come Again

Secondly, Jesus will come again. That is another reason for girding our loins, because it is clear that He has not quit the fight or deserted the field of battle. Our great Captain is still heading the conflict. He has ridden into another part of the field, but He will be back again, perhaps in the twinkling of an eye. You do not say that a commander has given up the campaign because it is expedient that he should withdraw from your part of the field. Our Lord did the best thing for His kingdom in going away. It was expedient to the highest degree that He should go and that we should each one receive the Spirit. There is a blessed unity between Christ the King and the most common soldier in the ranks. He has not taken His heart, His care, or His interest from us. He is bound up heart and soul with His people and their holy warfare, and this is the evidence of it:

"Behold, I come quickly; and my reward is with me, to give every man according as his work shall be" (Revelation 22:12).

Returning in the Same Manner

Moreover, we are told in the text—and this a reason why we should get to our work—that He is coming in like manner as He departed. Certain of the commentators do not seem to understand English at all. *"This same Jesus, which is taken up from you into heaven, shall so come in like manner as ye have seen him go into heaven."* This, they say, relates to His spiritual coming at Pentecost. Give anybody a grain of sense, and do they not see that a spiritual coming is not a coming *"in like manner"* as He went up into heaven? There is an analogy, but certainly not a likeness, between the two things. Our Lord was taken up; they could see Him rise. He will come again, and *"every eye shall see him"* (Revelation 1:7). He went up not in spirit, but in bodily form: likewise, He will come down bodily.

"This same Jesus...shall so come in like manner." He went up as a matter of fact—not in poetic figure and spiritual symbol, but as a matter of fact. *"This same Jesus"* literally went up, and He will literally come again. He will descend in clouds even as He went up in clouds, and *"he shall stand at the latter day upon the earth"* (Job 19:25) even as He stood before.

He went up to heaven unopposed; no high priests, or scribes, or Pharisees, or even one of the rabble opposed His Ascension. It is ridiculous to suppose that they could. When He comes a second time, none will stand against Him. His adversaries will perish; as the fat of rams, they will melt away in His presence. When He comes, He will break rebellious nations with a rod of iron (see Revelation 2:26–27), for His force will be irresistible in that day.

Beloved, do not let anybody spiritualize away all this from you. Jesus is coming as a matter of fact; therefore, go to your sphere of service as a matter of fact. Get to work and teach the ignorant, win the wayward, instruct the children, and everywhere tell out the sweet name of Jesus. As a matter of fact, give of your substance, but do not talk about your giving. As a matter of fact, consecrate your daily life to the glory of God. As a matter of fact, live wholly for your Redeemer. Jesus is not coming in a sort of mythical, misty, hazy way. He is literally and actually coming, and He will literally and actually call upon you to give an account of your stewardship. Therefore, today, literally and not symbolically, personally and not by deputy, go out through the portion of the world that you can reach *and preach the gospel to every creature* (Mark 16:15), as you have opportunity.

Be Ready to Meet Him

This is what the men in white apparel meant —be ready to meet your coming Lord. What is the way to be ready to meet Jesus? It is the same Jesus who went away from us who is coming, so then let us be doing what He was doing before He went away. If it is the same Jesus who is coming, we cannot possibly put ourselves into any posture of which He will better approve than by going about doing good. If you would meet Him with joy, serve Him with earnestness. If the Lord Jesus Christ were to come today, I would like Him to find me at my studying, praying, or preaching. Would you not like Him to find you in your Sunday school, in your class, or out there at the corner of the street preaching, or doing whatever you have the privilege of doing in His name? Would you meet your Lord in idleness? Do not think of it.

One morning I called to see a sister. When I arrived, she was cleaning the front steps with some whitening. She apologized very much and said that she felt ashamed of being caught in such a position. I replied, "Dear friend, you could not be in a better position than you are, for you are doing your duty as a good housewife. May God bless you." She had no money to spare for a servant, and she was doing her duty by keeping the home tidy. I thought she looked more beautiful with her pail beside her than if she had been dressed according to the latest fashion. I said to her, "I assure you that I would like my Lord to come and find me, just as I have found you, doing my daily work with all my heart and fulfilling the duty of the hour. May the Lord Jesus Christ, when He comes suddenly, find you just as you are, doing your duty!"

I want you all to get to your pails without being ashamed of them. Serve the Lord in some way or other. Serve Him always; serve Him intensely; serve Him more and more. Go tomorrow and serve the Lord at the counter, in the workshop, or in the field. Go and serve the Lord by helping the poor and the needy, the widow and the fatherless. Serve Him by teaching the children, but especially by endeavoring to train your own children. Go and hold a temperance meeting; show the drunkard that there is hope for Him in Christ. Go to the midnight meeting, and let the fallen woman know that Jesus can restore her.

Do what Jesus has given you the power to do. Then, Christian disciples, you will not stand gazing up into heaven, but you will wait upon the Lord in prayer, receive the Spirit of God, and publish to all around the doctrine of "believe and live." Then, when Christ comes, He will say to you, *"Well done, good and faithful servant...enter thou into the joy of thy lord"* (Matthew 25:23). So may His grace enable us to do. Amen.

Chapter Four

Coming Judgment of the Secrets of Men

In the day when God shall judge the secrets of men
by Jesus Christ according to my gospel.
—Romans 2:16

I t is impossible for any of us to tell what it cost
the apostle Paul to write the first chapter of
the epistle to the Romans. *"It is a shame even
to speak of those things which are done* [by the vicious] *in secret"* (Ephesians 5:12), but Paul felt
that it was necessary to break through his shame
and to speak out concerning the hideous vices of
the heathen. He has left on record an exposure of
the sins of his day, which crimsons the cheeks of
the modest when they read it and makes the ears
of him that hears it tingle.

Paul knew that this chapter would be read,
not in his age alone, but in all ages, and that it
would go into the households of the most pure and
godly as long as the world should stand. Yet he
deliberately wrote it, and wrote it under the guidance of the Holy Spirit. He knew that it must be

written to put to shame the abominations of an age which was almost past shame. Monsters that revel in darkness must be dragged into the open so that they may be withered up by the light.

After Paul had thus written in anguish, he thought about his chief comfort. While his pen was black with the words he had written in the first chapter, he was driven to write about his greatest delight. He held on to the Gospel with a greater tenacity than ever. As in this verse, he needed to mention the Gospel. He did not speak of it as "the Gospel" but as *"my gospel." "God shall judge the secrets of men by Jesus Christ according to my gospel."*

Paul must have felt that he could not live in the midst of such depraved people without holding the Gospel with both hands and grasping it as his very own. *"My gospel,"* said he. Not that Paul was the author of it, not that Paul had an exclusive monopoly of its blessings, but that he had so received it from Christ Himself and regarded himself as so responsibly entrusted with it that he could not disown it even for an instant. So fully had he taken it into himself that he could not do less than call it *"my gospel."* In other places he spoke of *"our gospel"* (2 Corinthians 4:3; 1 Thessalonians 1:5; 2 Thessalonians 2:14), thus using a possessive pronoun to show how believers identify themselves with the truth that they preach.

Paul had a Gospel, a definite form of truth, and he believed in it beyond all doubt. Therefore, he spoke of it as *"my gospel."* We can hear the voice of faith that seems to say, "Though others reject it, I am sure of it and allow no shade of mistrust to darken my mind. To me it is *'good tidings of great joy'* (Luke 2:10): I hail it as *'my gospel.'* If I am called a fool for holding on to it, I am content to be a fool and to find all my wisdom in my Lord."

> Should all the forms that men devise
>> Assault my faith with treacherous art,
> I'd call them vanity and lies,
>> And bind the Gospel to my heart.

Is not this word, *"my gospel,"* the voice of love? Does he not by this word embrace the Gospel as the only love of his soul, for the sake of which he had suffered the loss of all things and counted them but dung (Philippians 3:8), for the sake of which he was willing to stand before Nero and proclaim the message from heaven, even in Caesar's palace? Though each word should cost him a life, he was willing to die a thousand deaths in the holy cause. *"My gospel,"* said he, with a rapture of delight, as he pressed to his bosom the sacred deposit of truth.

"My gospel." Does not this show his courage? It is as much as to say, *"I am not ashamed of the gospel of Christ: for it is the power of God unto salvation to every one that believeth"* (Romans 1:16). He said *"my gospel,"* as a soldier speaks of "my colors" or of "my king." He resolves to bear this banner to victory and to serve this royal truth even to the death.

"My gospel." There is a touch of discrimination about the expression. Paul perceived that

there were other gospels being promoted, and he made short work of them when he said,

[8] *But though we, or an angel from heaven, preach any other gospel unto you than that which we have preached unto you, let him be accursed.* (Galatians 1:8)

The apostle had a gentle spirit. He prayed heartily for the Jews who persecuted him and yielded his life for the conversion of the Gentiles who maltreated him, but he had no tolerance for those who preached a false gospel. He exhibited great breadth of mind, and to save souls he became all things to all men (1 Corinthians 9:22). However, when he contemplated any alteration or adulteration of the Gospel of Christ, he thundered and lightninged without measure. When he feared that something else might spring up among the philosophers or among the Judaizers that would hide a single beam of the glorious Sun of Righteousness, he used no measured language, but cried concerning the author of such a darkening influence, *"Let him be accursed."*

Every heart that would see men blessed whispers an "Amen" to the apostolic benediction. No greater curse can come upon mankind than the obscuring of the Gospel of Jesus Christ. Paul said of himself and his true brothers and sisters, *"We are not as many, which corrupt the word of God"* (2 Corinthians 2:17). He cried to those who turned aside from the one, true Gospel, *"O foolish Galatians, who hath bewitched you?"* (Galatians 3:1).

He spoke of all new doctrines as *"another gospel: which is not another; but there be some that trouble you"* (Galatians 1:6–7).

As for myself, looking at the matter afresh, amid all the filthiness that I see in the world of this day, I lay hold upon the pure and blessed Word of God and call it all the more earnestly, *"my gospel"*—mine in life and mine in death, mine against all comers, mine forever, with God helping me. With emphasis I say, *"my gospel."*

Now let us notice what it was that brought up this expression, *"my gospel."* What was Paul preaching about? Certainly not about any of the gentle and tender themes which we are told nowadays ought to occupy all our time. Rather, he was speaking of the terrors of the law, and in that connection he spoke of *"my gospel."*

Let us at once turn our attention to this text. It needs no dividing, for it divides itself. First, let us consider that on a certain day, God will judge mankind; secondly, on that day God will judge the secrets of men; thirdly, when He judges the secrets of men, it will be by Jesus Christ; and, fourthly, this judgment is according to the Gospel.

God Will Certainly Judge

We begin with the solemn truth that on a certain day God will judge men. A judgment is going on daily. God is continually holding court and considering the behavior of the sons of men. Every evil deed that they do is recorded in the register of doom, and each good action is remembered and laid up in store by God. That judgment is reflected in a measure in the consciences of men. Those who know the Gospel, and those who know it not, have a certain measure of light alike, by which they know right from wrong—their consciences are all the while accusing or else excusing them.

This session of the heavenly court continues from day to day like that of our local magistrates. This does not prevent, but rather necessitates, the holding of an ultimate great judgment. As each man passes into another world, there is an immediate judgment passed upon him, but this is only the foreshadowing of that which will take place at the end of the age.

There is a judgment also passing upon nations. Since nations will not exist as nations in another world, they have to be judged and punished in this present state. The thoughtful reader of history will not fail to observe how sternly justice has dealt with empire after empire when they have become corrupt. Colossal dominions have withered when sentenced by the King of Kings. Ask yourself, "Where is the empire of Assyria today? Where are the mighty cities of Babylon? Where are the glories of the Medes and Persians? What has become of the Macedonian power? Where are the Caesars and their palaces?" These empires were forces established by cruelty and used for oppression; they fostered luxury and licentiousness. When they were no longer tolerable, the earth was purged from their polluting existence. What horrors of war, bloodshed, and devastation have come upon men as the result of their iniquities!

The world is full of the monuments, both of the mercy and the justice of God. In fact, the monuments of His justice, if rightly viewed, are proofs of His goodness: it is mercy on the part of God to put an end to evil systems when, like a nightmare, they weigh heavily upon the shoulders of mankind.

The omnipotent Judge has not ceased from His sovereign rule over kingdoms, and our own country may yet have to feel His chastisements. We have often laughed among ourselves at the ridiculous idea of the New Zealander sitting on the broken arch of London Bridge amid the ruins of this metropolis. However, is it quite so ridiculous as it looks? It is more than possible that it will be realized if our iniquities continue to abound. What is there about London that it should be more enduring than Rome? Why should the palaces of our monarchs be eternal if the palaces of Russia have fallen? The almost boundless power of the Pharaohs has passed away, and Egypt has become the lowliest of nations. Why should not England come under like condemnation? What are we? What is there about our boastful race, whether on this side of the Atlantic or the other, that we should monopolize the favor of God? If we rebel and sin against Him, He will not hold us guiltless, but will deal out impartial justice to an ungrateful race.

Still, though such judgments proceed every day, yet there is to be a day in which God will judge the sons of men in a more distinct, formal, public, and final manner. We might have guessed this by the light of nature and of reason. Even heathen people have had a dim notion of a day of doom. However, we are not left to guess it; we are solemnly assured of it in Holy Scripture. Accepting this Book as the revelation of God, we know beyond all doubt that a day is appointed in which the Lord *"shall judge the secrets of men."*

Judging in this context means all that concerns the proceedings of trial and verdict. God will judge the race of men. That is to say, first, there will be a session of majesty and the appearing of a Great White Throne, surrounded with the pomp of angels and glorified beings. Then, a summons will be issued, bidding all men to come to judgment, to give their final accounts. The heralds will fly through the realms of death and summon those who sleep in the dust, for the quick and the dead *"must all appear before that judgment seat of Christ"* (2 Corinthians 5:10). John said,

^{12} *I saw the dead, small and great, stand before God...*
^{13} *And the sea gave up the dead which were in it; and death and hell delivered up the dead which were in them.* (Revelation 20:12–13)

Those who have been buried for so long that their dust is mingled with the soil and have undergone a thousand transmutations will nevertheless be made to appear personally before the judgment seat of Christ. What an inquest that will be! You and I and all the myriads of our race will be gathered before the throne of the Son of God. Then, when all are gathered, the indictment will be read, and each one will be examined concerning *"the things done in his body, according to that he hath done, whether it be good or bad"* (2 Corinthians 5:10). Then the books will be opened, and everything recorded there will be read before the face of heaven. Every sinner will then hear the story of his life published to his everlasting shame. The good will ask no concealment, and the evil will find none. Angels and men will then see the truth of things, and the saints will judge the world.

The great Judge Himself will then give the decision: He will pronounce sentence upon the wicked and execute their punishment. No partiality will be seen. There will be no private conferences to secure immunity for nobles, no hushing up of matters so that great men may escape contempt for their crimes. All men will stand before the one great judgment bar. Evidence will be given concerning them all, and a righteous sentence shall go forth from His mouth who knows not how to flatter the great.

This will be so, and it ought to be so. God should judge the world because He is the universal Ruler and Sovereign. There has been a day for sinning; there ought to be a day for punishing. A long age of rebellion has been endured; there must be a time when justice asserts her supremacy. We have seen an age in which reformation has been commanded, in which mercy has been presented, in which dissuasion and entreaty have been used. There ought at last to come a day when God *"shall judge the quick and the dead"* (2 Timothy 4:1) and measure to each the final result of life.

It ought to be so for the sake of the righteous. They have been slandered, despised, and ridiculed. Worse than that, they have been imprisoned, beaten, and put to death times without number. The best have had the worst of it, and there ought to be a judgment to set these things right.

Besides, the festering iniquities of each age cry out to God that He should deal with them. Shall such sin go unpunished? To what end is there a moral government at all, and how is its continuance to be secured, if there are not rewards and punishments and a day of reckoning? For the display of His holiness, for the overwhelming of His adversaries, for the rewarding of those who have faithfully served Him, there must be and shall be a day in which God will judge the world.

Why does it not come at once? And when will it come? The precise date we cannot tell. Neither man nor angel knows that day, and it is idle and profane to guess at it since even the Son of Man does not know the time (Matthew 24:36).

It is sufficient for us that the Judgment Day will surely come; it ought to be sufficient also to believe that it is postponed on purpose to give breathing time for mercy and space for repentance. Why should the ungodly want to know when that day will come? What is that day to them? To them it will be darkness, not light. It will be the day of their being consumed as completely dry stubble. Therefore, bless the Lord that He delays His coming, and know that *"the longsuffering of our Lord is* [for the] *salvation"* (2 Peter 2:3) of many.

Moreover, the Lord keeps the scaffold standing until He has built up the fabric of His church. Not yet are the elect all called out from among the guilty sons of men. Not yet have all the redeemed with blood been redeemed with power and brought forth out of the corruption of the age into the holiness in which they walk with God. Therefore, the Lord waits.

However, do not deceive yourselves. The great day of His wrath is coming, and your days of reprieve are numbered. *"One day is with the Lord as a thousand years, and a thousand years as one day"* (2 Peter 3:8). Perhaps you may die before the appearing of the Son of Man, but, even so, you will see His judgment seat, for you will rise again as surely as He rose. When the apostle Paul addressed the Grecian sages at Athens, he said,

> [30] *God...now commandeth all men every where to repent:*
> [31] *Because he hath appointed a day, in the which he will judge the world in righteousness by that man whom he hath ordained; whereof he hath given assurance unto all men, in that he hath raised him from the dead.* (Acts 17:30–31)

Do you not see, O you impenitent ones, that a risen Savior is the sign of your doom? As God has raised Jesus from the dead, so He will raise your bodies, that in these you may come to judgment. Before the judgment seat every man and woman will give an account of the things done in the body, whether they be good or whether they be evil. (See Romans 14:12; 2 Corinthians 5:10.) Thus the Lord has decreed, and thus it shall be so.

The Secrets of Men Will Be Judged

Now, I want to call your attention to the idea that *"God shall judge the secrets of men."* This will happen to all men, of every nation, of every age, of every rank, and of every character. The Judge will, of course, judge their outward acts, but these may be said to have preceded them to judgment. Their secret acts are specially mentioned, because these will make judgment all the more searching.

By *"the secrets of men,"* the Scripture means those secret crimes that hide themselves away by their own infamy, which are too vile to be spoken of, which cause a shudder to go through a nation if they are dragged, as they ought to be, into the daylight. Secret offenses will be brought into judgment. The deeds of the night and of the closed room, the acts that require the finger to be laid upon the lip and a conspiracy of silence to be sworn, revolting and shameless sins that must never be mentioned lest the man who committed them be excluded from his fellowmen as an outcast and abhorred even by other sinners—all these will be revealed.

All that any of you have done or are doing, if you are bearing the Christian name and yet practicing secret sin, will be laid bare before the universal gaze. If you sit among the people of God but you are living in dishonesty, untruthfulness, or uncleanness when no other eye can see, it will all be known. Shame and confusion of face will eternally cover you. Contempt will be the inheritance to which you awake when hypocrisy is no more possible. *"Be not deceived; God is not mocked: for whatsoever a man soweth, that shall He also reap"* (Galatians 6:7). He will bring the secrets of men into judgment.

Our text especially refers to the hidden motives of every action. A man may do that which is right from a wrong motive, and so the deed may be evil in the sight of God, though it seems right in the sight of men. Oh, think what it will be to have your motives all brought to light, to have it proven that you were godly for the sake of gain, that you were generous out of ostentation or zealous for love of praise, that you were careful in public to maintain a religious reputation but that all the while everything was done for self and self only! What a strong light will that be which God will turn upon our lives, when the darkest chambers of human desire and motive will be as manifest as public acts! What a revelation it will be that makes manifest all thoughts, imaginings, lusts, and desires! All angers, envies, prides, and rebellions of the heart—what a disclosure will these make! All the sensual desires and imaginings of even the best-regulated—what a foulness will these appear! What a day it will be when the secrets of men will be set in the full blaze of noon!

God will also reveal secrets that were secrets even to the sinners themselves, for there is sin in us that we have never seen and iniquity in us that we have never yet discovered. For our own comfort's sake, we have managed to blind our eyes somewhat, and we take care to avert our gaze from things that are inconvenient to see. However, we will be compelled to see all these evils in that day, when the Lord *"shall judge the secrets of men."*

I do not wonder that when a certain rabbi read in the book of Ecclesiastes, *"For God shall bring every work into judgment, with every secret thing, whether it be good, or whether it be evil"* (v. 12:14), that he wept. It is enough to make the best man tremble. Were it not for You, Jesus, whose precious blood has cleansed us from all sin, where would we be? Were it not for Your righteousness, which covers those who believe in You, who among us could endure the thought of that tremendous day? In You, Jesus, we are made righteous, and therefore we fear not the trial hour. But were it not for You, our hearts would fail us for fear!

Now, if you ask me why God should specially judge the secrets of men—since this is not done in human courts, and cannot be, for secret things of this kind come not under cognizance of our short-sighted tribunals—I answer it is because there is really nothing secret from God. We make a difference between secret and public sins, but He does not, for all things are naked and open to His eyes. All deeds are done in the immediate presence of God, who is personally present everywhere. He knows and sees all things as one, and every secret sin is but conceived to be secret through the deluded fantasy of our ignorance. God sees more of a secret sin than any man can see of that which is done before his face. *"Can any hide himself in secret places that I shall not see him? saith the LORD"* (Jeremiah 23:24).

The secrets of men will be judged because often the greatest of moral acts are done in secret. The brightest deeds that God delights in are those that are done by His servants when they have shut the door and are alone with Him, when they have no motive but to please Him, when they studiously avoid publicity lest they should be turned aside by the praise of men, when the right hand knows not what the left hand does (Matthew 6:3), and when the loving, generous heart devises liberal things (Isaiah 32:8) and does them confidentially so that it should never be discovered how the deed was done. It would be a pity that such deeds should be left out at the great audit.

Thus, too, secret vices are also of the very blackest kind, and to exempt them would be to let the worst of sinners go unpunished. Should it be that these polluted beings would escape because they have purchased silence with their wealth? I say solemnly, *"God forbid"* (Romans 3:6). And He does forbid it. What they have done in secret will be proclaimed from the housetops.

Besides, the secret things of men enter into the very essence of their actions. An action is, after all, good or bad very much according to its motive. It may seem good, but the heart's incentive may taint it. Thus, if God did not judge the secret part of an action, He would not judge righteously. He will weigh all our actions, detect the designs that led to them, and reveal the motives that prompted them.

Is it not certainly true that the secret thing is the best evidence of the man's condition? Many a man will not do in public what would bring him shame, not because he is not black-hearted enough for it, but because he is too much of a coward. That which a man does when he thinks that he is entirely by himself is the best revelation of the man. That which you will not do because it would be told of you if you did ill is a poor index of your real character. That which you will do because you will be praised for doing well is an equally faint test of your heart. Such virtue is mere self-seeking, or mean-spirited, subservience to your fellowman. However, that which you do out of respect to no authority but your own conscience and your God, that which you do unobserved, without regard to what man will say concerning it—such actions reveal you and discover your real soul. Hence, God lays a special stress and emphasis here upon the fact that He will in that day *"judge the secrets of men by Jesus Christ."*

Oh, friends, if it does not make you tremble to think of these things, it ought to do so. I feel the deep responsibility of emphasizing such matters, and I pray that God in His infinite mercy will apply these truths to our hearts that they may be forceful in our lives. These truths ought to startle us, but I am afraid we come in contact with them with small result. We have grown familiar with them, and they do not penetrate us as they should. We have to deal, beloved, with an omniscient God, with One who never forgets what is known, with One to whom all things are always present, with

One who will conceal nothing out of fear or favor of any person, with One who will shortly bring the splendor of His omniscience and the impartiality of His justice to bear upon all human lives. God help us, wherever we rove and wherever we rest, to remember that each thought, word, and act of each moment lies in that fierce light which beats upon all things from the throne of God.

Judged by Jesus Christ

Another solemn revelation of our text lies in the fact that *"God shall judge the secrets of men by Jesus Christ."* He that will sit upon the throne as God's Vice General and as the Judge, acting for God, will be Jesus Christ. What a name for a judge—the Savior-Anointed, Jesus Christ! He is to be the Judge of all mankind. Our Redeemer will be the determiner of our destiny.

In the first place, I do not doubt that this will be for the display of His glory. What a difference there will be then between the babe of Bethlehem's manger, who was hunted by Herod and carried down by night into Egypt for shelter, and the King of Kings and Lord of Lords before whom every knee must bow! What a difference between the weary man, full of woes, and He who will then be clothed with glory, sitting on a throne encircled with a rainbow! From the derision of men to the throne of universal judgment, what an ascent!

I am unable to convey to you my own heart's sense of the contrast between the Son of Man who *"is despised and rejected of men"* (Isaiah 53:3) and the universally-acknowledged Lord, before whom Caesars and pontiffs will bow in the dust. He who was judged at Pilate's bar will summon all to His bar. What a change from the shame and spitting, from the nails and the wounds, from the mockery and the thirst, from the dying anguish, to the glory in which will come He whose eyes are as a flame of fire and out of whose mouth there goes a two-edged sword (Revelation 1:14, 16)! *"And he shall judge among the nations, and shall rebuke many people"* (Isaiah 2:4), even He whom the nations abhorred. He will break them in pieces like a potter's vessel, even those who cast Him out as unworthy to live among them.

Oh, how we ought to bow before Him now as He reveals Himself in His tender sympathy and in His generous humiliation! Let us *"kiss the Son, lest he be angry"* (Psalm 2:12). Let us yield to His grace, that we may not be crushed by His wrath. You sinners, bow before those pierced feet, or else they will tread you like clusters in the winepress. Look up to Him with weeping, confess your forgetfulness of Him, and put your trust in Him, lest He look down on you in indignation. Remember that He will one day say, *"Those mine enemies, which would not that I should reign over them, bring hither, and slay them before me"* (Luke 19:27).

The holding of the judgment by the Lord Jesus will greatly enhance His glory. It will finally settle one controversy which is still upheld by certain erring spirits: no doubt will remain as to our Lord's deity in that day—no question that *"this same Jesus"* (Acts 1:11) who was crucified is both

Lord and God. God Himself will judge, but He will perform the judgment in the person of His Son Jesus Christ, truly man, but nevertheless most truly God. Being God, He is divinely qualified to *"judge the world with righteousness, and the people with his truth"* (Psalm 96:13).

You again ask, "Why is the Son of God chosen to be the final Judge?" I give as a further answer that He receives this high office not only as a reward for all His pains and as a manifestation of His glory, but also because men have been under His mediatorial sway and He is their Governor and King. At the present moment, we are all under the sway of the Prince Immanuel, God with us. We have been placed by an act of divine clemency, not under the immediate government of an offended God, but under the reconciling rule of the Prince of Peace. Jesus said, *"All power is given unto me in heaven and in earth"* (Matthew 28:18). *"For the Father judgeth no man, but hath committed all judgment unto the Son: That all men should honour the Son, even as they honour the Father"* (John 5:22-23). We are commanded *"to preach unto the people, and to testify that it is he which was ordained of God to be the judge of quick and dead"* (Acts 10:42). Jesus is our Lord and King, and it is right that He should conclude His mediatorial sovereignty by rewarding His subjects according to their deeds.

I have something to express to you that ought to reach your hearts even if other thoughts have not done so. I think that God has chosen Christ, the man Christ Jesus, to judge the world so that there may never be a quibble raised concerning that judgment. Men will not be able to say, "We were judged by a superior being who did not know our weaknesses and temptations, and therefore He judged us harshly and without a generous consideration of our condition." No, *"God shall judge the secrets of men by Jesus Christ,"* who *"was in all points tempted like as we are, yet without sin"* (Hebrews 4:15). He is our brother, bone of our bone and flesh of our flesh, partaker of our humanity, and therefore understands and knows what is in men. He has shown Himself to be skillful in all the surgery of mercy throughout the ages. At last He will be found equally skillful in dissecting motives and revealing the thoughts and intents of the heart. Nobody will ever be able to look back on that imposing tribunal and say that He who sat upon it was too stern because He knew nothing of human weakness. It will be the loving Christ, whose tears and bloody sweat and gaping wounds attest to His brotherhood with mankind. It will be clear to all intelligence that however dreadful His sentences, He could not be unmerciful. *"God shall judge* [us] *by Jesus Christ,"* in order that the judgment may be indisputable.

But pay close attention, for I write with a great weight upon my soul. This judgment *"by Jesus Christ"* puts beyond possibility all hope of any post-intervention. If the Savior condemns, who can plead for us? In a parable found in the thirteenth chapter of Luke, Jesus told of an owner of a vineyard who was about to cut down a barren fig tree when the dresser of the vineyard pleaded,

"Let it alone another year." But what can come of that tree when the vinedresser himself says to the master, "It must fall; I myself must cut it down"? When your Savior becomes your Judge, you will be judged indeed. If He should say, *"Depart from me, ye cursed"* (Matthew 25:41), who can call you back? If He that bled to save men at last comes to this conclusion—that there is no more to be done but they must be driven from His presence—then bid farewell to all hope. To the guilty, the judgment will indeed be a

Great day of dread, decision, and despair.

An infinite horror will seize upon their spirits as the words of the loving Christ freeze the very marrow of their bones and fix them in the ice of eternal despair. There is, to my mind, a climax of solemnity in the fact that *"God shall judge the secrets of men by Jesus Christ."*

Does not this also show how certain the sentence will be? This Christ of God is too much in earnest to play with men. If He says, *"Come, ye blessed of my Father"* (Matthew 25:34), He will not fail to bring them to their inheritance. If He is driven to say, *"Depart from me, ye cursed,"* He will see it is done, and into the everlasting punishment they must go. Even when it cost Him His life, He did not draw back from doing the will of His Father, nor will He shrink in that day when He pronounces the sentence of doom. Oh, how evil must sin be since it constrains the tender Savior to pronounce sentence of eternal woe!

I am sure that many of us have been driven lately to an increased hatred of sin, and our souls have recoiled within us because of the wickedness amid which we dwell. It has made us feel as if we would gladly borrow the Almighty's thunderbolts with which to smite iniquity. Such haste on our parts may not be seemly, since it implies a complaint against divine long-suffering. But Christ's dealing with evil will be calm and dispassionate, and all the more crushing. Jesus, with His pierced hand that attests of His supreme love to men, will wave the impenitent away. Those lips which bade the weary to rest in Him will solemnly say to the wicked, *"Depart from me, ye cursed, into everlasting fire, prepared for the devil and his angels"* (Matthew 25:41). To be trampled beneath the foot that was nailed to the cross will be to be crushed indeed. Yet, so it is that *"God shall judge the secrets of men by Jesus Christ."*

In God's judging men *"by Jesus Christ,"* it seems to me as if God intended to give a display of the unity of all His perfection. In this same man, Christ Jesus, the Son of God, you behold justice and love, mercy and righteousness, combined in equal measure. He turns to the right and says, *"Come, ye blessed"* (Matthew 25:34), with infinite grace; with the same lip, as He glances to the left, He says, *"Depart from me, ye cursed."* Men will then see at one glance how love and righteousness are one, and how they meet in equal splendor in the person of the Well-beloved, whom God has therefore chosen *"to be the Judge of quick and dead"* (Acts 10:42).

I will finish this subject with my last point, which is that all of this is according to the Gospel. What I am attempting to express is that there is nothing in the Gospel contrary to this solemn teaching. Men gather to us to hear us preach of infinite mercy and tell of the love that blots out sin. The task is joyful when we are called to deliver such a message. But, remember, nothing in that message makes light of sin. The Gospel offers you no opportunity of going on in sin and escaping without punishment. Its own cry is, *"Except ye repent, ye shall all likewise perish"* (Luke 13:3, 5).

Jesus did not come into the world to make sin less terrible. Nothing in the Gospel excuses sin; nothing in it affords toleration for lust or anger, dishonesty or falsehood. The Gospel is as truly a two-edged sword against sin as ever the law can be. There is grace for the man who repents from his sin, but there is tribulation and wrath upon every man that does evil. *"If* [you] *turn not, he will whet his sword; he hath bent his bow, and made it ready"* (Psalm 7:12).

The Gospel is all tenderness to the repenting, but all terror to the obstinate offender. It has pardon for the very chief of sinners and mercy for the vilest of the vile, if they will forsake their sins; but it is according to our Gospel that he who goes on in his iniquity will be cast into hell and *"he that believeth not shall be damned"* (Mark 16:16). With deep love for the souls of men, I bear witness to the truth that he who turns not with repentance and faith to Christ, will go away into punishment as everlasting as the life of the righteous. This is according to our Gospel. Indeed, we would not have needed such a Gospel if there had not been such a judgment. The background of the Cross is the judgment seat of Christ. We would not have needed so great an atonement, so vast a sacrifice, if there had not been a supreme sinfulness in sin, a transcendent justice in the judgment, and an incomparable terror in the sure rewards of transgression.

"According to my gospel," said Paul; he meant that the judgment is an essential part of the gospel creed. If I had to sum up the Gospel, I should have to tell you certain facts: Jesus, the Son of God, became man; He was born of the Virgin Mary; He lived a perfect life; He was falsely accused of men; He was crucified, died, and was buried; the third day He rose again from the dead; He ascended into heaven and sits on the right hand of God, from where He will also come to judge the quick and the dead. These are the elementary truths of our Gospel. We believe in the resurrection of the dead, the final judgment, and the life everlasting.

The judgment is according to the Gospel. In times of righteous indignation, its terrible significance seems to be the Gospel in itself to the pure in heart. I mean this: As I have read information concerning oppression, slavery, the treading down of the poor, and the shedding of blood, I have rejoiced that there is a righteous Judge. I have read of secret wickedness among the rich men of this city, and I have said to myself, "Thank God, there will be a Judgment Day." Thousands of men have been hanged for lesser crimes than those which are now being committed by gentlemen whose names are on the lips of rank and beauty. Ah, me, how heavy is my heart as I think of it! It has come the Gospel to me that the Lord will be revealed *"in flaming fire taking vengeance on them that know not God, and that obey not the gospel of our Lord Jesus Christ"* (2 Thessalonians 1:8). The secret wickedness of London cannot go on forever. Even they who truly love men and most desire salvation for them cannot but cry out, "How long? How long, O God? Will You endure this forever?" God has appointed a day when He will judge the world; we sigh and cry until it ends the reign of wickedness and give rests to the oppressed.

Beloved, we must preach the coming of the Lord, and preach it more than we have done, because it is the driving power of the Gospel. Too many have kept back these truths, and thus the bone has been taken out of the arm of the Gospel. Its point has been broken; its edge has been blunted. The doctrine of judgment to come is the power by which men are to be aroused. There is another life, the Lord will come a second time, judgment will arrive, and the wrath of God will be revealed. Where this is not preached, I am bold to say, the Gospel is not preached. It is absolutely necessary to the preaching of the Gospel of Christ that men be warned as to what will happen if they continue in their sins.

Surgeon, are you too delicate to tell the man that he is ill? Do you hope to heal the sick without their knowing it? If you therefore flatter them, what happens? They laugh at you, they dance upon their own graves, and at last they die! Your delicacy is cruelty; your flatteries are poisons; you are a murderer. Should we ministers keep men in a fool's paradise? Should we lull them into soft slumbers from which they will awake in hell? Are we to become helpers of their damnation by our smooth speeches? In the name of God, we dare not. It becomes every true minister of Christ to cry aloud and spare not, for God has set a day in which He will *judge the secrets of men by Jesus Christ according to my gospel.*

As surely as Paul's Gospel was true, the judgment will come. Therefore, flee to Jesus this day, O sinners. O you saints, come hide yourselves again beneath the crimson canopy of the atoning sacrifice, so that you may now be ready to welcome your descending Lord and escort Him to His judgment seat. O my beloved, may God bless you, for Jesus' sake. Amen.

Chapter Five

The Two Appearings and the Discipline of Grace

For the grace of God that bringeth salvation hath
appeared to all men, Teaching us that, denying
ungodliness and worldly lusts, we should live soberly,
righteously, and godly, in this present world;
Looking for that blessed hope,
and the glorious appearing of the great God
and our Saviour Jesus Christ;
Who gave himself for us, that he might
redeem us from all iniquity, and purify unto himself
a peculiar people, zealous of good works.
—Titus 2:11–14

U pon reading this text, we see at a glance that Paul believed in the divinity of our Savior. He did not preach a savior who was a mere man. He believed the Lord Jesus Christ to be truly man, but he also believed Him to be God over all, and he thus used the striking words, *"the glorious appearing of the great God and our Saviour Jesus Christ."* There is no appearing of God the Father; no such expression is found in Scripture. This appearing is the appearing of that second person of the blessed Trinity, who has already appeared once and who will *"appear the second time without sin unto salvation"* (Hebrews 9:28) in the latter days.

Paul believed in Jesus as *"the great God and our Saviour."* It was his high delight to extol the Lord who once was crucified in weakness. He calls Him here, *"the great God,"* thus especially dwelling upon His power, dominion, and glory. This is all the more remarkable because he immediately went on to say, *"who gave himself for us, that he might redeem us from all iniquity."* He who gave Himself, He who surrendered life itself upon the accursed tree, He who was stripped of all honor and glory and entered into the utmost depths of humiliation—He was most assuredly the great God, all of that notwithstanding. O beloved, if you take away the deity of Christ, what in the Gospel is left that is worth preaching? None but *"the great God"* is equal to the work of being our Savior.

We learn also at first sight that Paul believed in a great redemption. *"Who gave himself for us, that he might redeem us from all iniquity."* That word *redemption* sounds in my ears like a silver bell. We are ransomed, purchased back from slavery, and this at an immeasurable price—not merely by the obedience of Christ, nor the suffering of Christ, nor even the death of Christ, but by Christ's giving Himself for us. All that there is in the great God and Savior was paid down in order *"that he might redeem us from all iniquity."*

The splendor of the Gospel lies in the redeeming sacrifice of the Son of God. It is the gem of all the gospel gems. As the moon is among the stars, so is this great doctrine among all the lesser lights that God has kindled to gladden the night of fallen man. Paul never hesitated; he had a divine Savior and a divine redemption, and he preached these with unwavering confidence. Oh, that all preachers were like him!

It is also clear that Paul looked upon the appearing of the Savior and Redeemer from all iniquity as a display of the grace of God. He said, *"For the grace of God that bringeth salvation hath appeared to all men."* In the person of Christ, the grace of God is revealed, as when the sun rises and makes glad all lands. It is not a private vision of God to a favored prophet on a lone mountaintop, but it is an open declaration of the grace of God to every creature under heaven, a display of the grace of God to all eyes that are open to behold it.

When the Lord Jesus Christ came to Bethlehem, and when He closed a perfect life by death upon Calvary, He manifested the grace of God more gloriously than has been done by creation or providence. This is the clearest revelation of the everlasting mercy of the living God. In the Redeemer we behold the unveiling of the Father's face or, might I say, the laying bare of the divine heart. This is the *"dayspring from on high* [who] *visited us"* (Luke 1:78), *"the Sun of righteousness* [who arose] *with healing in his wings"* (Malachi 4:2).

The grace of God has shone forth conspicuously and made itself visible to men of every rank in the person and work of the Lord Jesus. This was not given to us because of any deserving of ours; it is a manifestation of free, rich, undeserved grace, and of that grace in its fullness. The grace of God has been made manifest to the entire universe in the appearing of Jesus Christ our Lord.

The grand object of the manifestation of divine grace in Christ Jesus is to deliver men from the dominion of evil. The world in Paul's day was steeped in immorality, debauchery, ungodliness, bloodshed, and cruelty of every kind. I do not have the space at this point to give you even an outline sketch of the Roman world when Paul wrote this letter to Titus. We are bad enough now, but the outward manners and customs of that period were simply horrible. The spread of the Gospel has brought about a change for the better. In the days of the apostles, the favorite spectacles for holiday entertainment were the butcheries of men. Such was the general depravity that vices which we hardly dare to mention were defended and gloried in. In the midnight of the world's history, our Lord appeared to put away sin. The Lord Jesus Christ, who is the manifestation of the divine grace to men, came into the world to put an end to the unutterable tyranny of evil. His work and teaching are meant to uplift mankind at large, as well as to redeem His people from all iniquity and to sanctify them to Himself as His peculiar heritage.

Paul looked upon recovery from sin as being a wonderful proof of divine grace. He was not talking about a kind of grace that would leave men in sin, yet save them from its punishment. No, this salvation is salvation from sin. He was not referring to a free grace that winks at iniquity and makes nothing of transgression; rather, he was talking about a far greater grace that denounces the iniquity, condemns the transgression, and then delivers the victim of it from the habit that has brought him into bondage. Paul declared that the grace of God has shone upon the world in the work of Jesus in order that the darkness of its sin and ignorance may disappear and the brightness of holiness, righteousness, and peace may rule the day. May God send us to see these blessed results in every part of the world! May God make us to see them in ourselves! May we ourselves feel that the grace of God has appeared to us individually!

Our apostle wanted Titus to know that this grace was intended for all ranks of men: for the Cretans, who were *"alway[s] liars, evil beasts, slow bellies"* (Titus 1:12), and even for the most despised bond slaves (Titus 2:9), who were treated worse than dogs under the Roman Empire. To each one of us, whether rich or poor, prominent or obscure, the Gospel has come. Its design is that we may be delivered by it from all ungodliness and worldly lusts.

This being the general thrust of the text, I ask you to examine it more closely, while I try to show how the apostle stimulates us to holiness and urges us to overcome all evil. May the Holy Spirit bless our meditations!

OUR POSITION: IN BETWEEN

First of all, we find in this text Paul's description of our position. The people of God stand between two appearances. In the eleventh verse we read, *"The grace of God that bringeth salvation hath appeared to all men."* Then in the thirteenth verse, we find, *"Looking for that blessed hope, and the glorious appearing of the great God and our Savior Jesus Christ."* We live in an age which is an interval between two appearings of the Lord from heaven. Believers in Jesus are shut off from the old system of doing things by the first coming of our Lord. *"The times of this ignorance God winked at; but now commandeth all men every where to repent"* (Acts 17:30).

We are divided from the past by a wall of light, of which some of the building stones are Bethlehem, Gethsemane, and Calvary. We date from the birth of the Virgin Mary's Son: we begin with *Anno Domini* (in the year of our Lord). All the rest of time is before Christ and is marked off from the Christian era. Bethlehem's manger is our beginning. The chief landmark for all time to us is the wondrous life of Him who is the light of the world. We look to the appearing of the grace of God in the form of the lowly One of Nazareth, for our trust is there. We confide in *"the Word* [who] *was made flesh, and dwelt among us, (and we beheld his glory, the glory as of the only begotten of the Father,) full of grace and truth"* (John 1:14). The dense darkness of the heathen ages begins to be broken when we reach the first appearing, and the dawn of a glorious day begins.

Beloved, we look forward to a second appearing. Our outlook for the close of this present era is another appearing—an appearing of glory rather than of grace. After our Master ascended from the brow of Olivet, His disciples remained for a while in mute astonishment; but soon an angelic messenger reminded them of prophecy and promise by saying, *"Ye men of Galilee, why stand ye gazing up into heaven? this same Jesus, which is taken up from you into heaven, shall so come in like manner as ye have seen him go into heaven"* (Acts 1:11). We believe that our Lord in the fullness of time *"shall descend from heaven with a shout, with the voice of the archangel, and with the trump of God"* (1 Thessalonians 4:16).

> The Lord shall come! the earth shall quake;
>   The mountains to their center shake;
> And, withering from the vault of night,
>   The stars shall pale their feeble light.

This is the terminus of the present age. We look from that noble *Anno Domini,* in which He came the first time, to that greater *Anno Domini,* in which He will come a second time in all the splendor of His power to reign in righteousness and break the evil powers as with a rod of iron.

See, then, where we are: we are encompassed about, behind and before, with the appearings of our Lord. Behind us is our trust; before us is our hope. Behind us is the Son of God in humiliation; before us is the great God our Savior in His glory. To use an ecclesiastical term, we stand between two epiphanies: the first is the manifestation of the Son of God in human flesh in weakness and humility; the second is the manifestation of the same Son of God in all His power and glory. In what a position, then, do we saints stand! We have an era all to ourselves which begins and ends with the Lord's appearings.

In This Present Age

Our position is further described in the text, if you look at it, as being in this present world or age. We are living in the age which lies between the two blazing beacons of the divine appearings, and we are called to hasten from one to the other. The sacramental host of God's elect is marching on from the one appearing to the other with hasty feet. We have everything to hope for in the last appearing, as we have everything to trust to in the first appearing. We have now to wait with patient hope through the weary interval that intervenes.

Paul called it *"this present world."* This marks its fleeting nature. It is present, but it is scarcely future, because the Lord may come so soon and thus end it all. It is present now, but it will not be present long. It is but a little time, and He who shall come will come and will not tarry. Now, it is *"this present world."* Oh, how present it is! How sadly it surrounds us!

However, by faith we count these present things to be insubstantial as a dream. We look to the things which are not seen and not present as being real and eternal. We pass through this world as men on pilgrimage. We traverse an enemy's country. Going from one manifestation to another, we are as birds migrating on the wing from one region to another: there is no rest for us by the way. We are to keep ourselves as loose as we can from this country through which we make our pilgrim's way, because we are strangers and foreigners and here we have no continuing city. We hurry through this Vanity Fair: before us lies the Celestial City and the coming of the Lord who is the King thereof. As voyagers cross the Atlantic, and so pass from shore to shore, so do we speed over the waves of this ever-changing world to the gloryland of the bright appearing of our Lord and Savior Jesus Christ.

Already I have given to you, in this description of our position, the very best argument for a holy life. If it is true, my beloved, then you are not of the world even as Jesus is not of the world. If this is so—that before you blazes the supernatural splendor of the Second Advent and behind you burns the everlasting light of the Redeemer's first appearing—what manner of people ought you to be!

If, indeed, you are but journeying through this present world, do not allow your hearts to be defiled with its sins; do not learn the manner of speech of these aliens through whose country you are passing. Is it not written, *"The people shall dwell alone, and shall not be reckoned among the nations"* (Numbers 23:9)? *"Wherefore come out from among them, and be ye separate, saith the Lord, and touch not the unclean thing; and I will receive you, And will be a Father unto you, and ye shall be my sons and daughters, saith the Lord Almighty"* (2 Corinthians 6:17–18).

They that lived before the coming of Christ had responsibilities upon them, but not such as those which rest upon you who have seen the face of God in Jesus Christ, and who expect to see that face again. You live in light that renders their brightest knowledge a comparative darkness: therefore, *"walk as children of light"* (Ephesians 5:8). You stand between two mornings, between which there is no evening. The glory of the Lord has risen upon you once in the incarnation and atonement of Christ Jesus: that light is shining more and more. Soon there will come the perfect day that will be ushered in by the Second Advent. The sun will no more go down, but it will unveil itself and shed an indescribable splendor upon all hearts that look for it.

"Therefore...let us put on the armour of light" (Romans 13:12). What a grand expression! Helmet of light, breastplate of light, shoes of light— everything of light. What a knight must he be who is clad, not in steel, but in light, light that flashes confusion on his foes! There ought to be a holy light about you, O believer in Jesus, for there is the appearing of grace behind you and the appearing of glory before you. Two manifestations of God shine upon you. Like a wall of fire, the Lord's appearings are round about you; there ought to be a special glory of holiness in the midst. *"Let your light so shine before men, that they may see your good works, and glorify your Father which is in heaven"* (Matthew 5:16). That is the position of the righteous according to the text, and it furnishes a loud call to holiness.

Secondly, I have to call your attention to the instruction that is given to us by the grace of God which has appeared to all men. The King James Version reads this way: *"The grace of God that bringeth salvation hath appeared to all men, Teaching us that, denying ungodliness and worldly lusts, we should live soberly, righteously, and godly, in this present world."*

A better translation of this verse might be: "The grace of God that brings salvation has appeared to all men, disciplining us in order that we may deny ungodliness and worldly lusts." Those of you who know a little Greek will note that the word that is rendered "teaching" in this version is a scholastic term and has to do with the education of children—not merely the teaching, but the training and bringing them up. The grace of God has come to be a schoolmaster to us, to teach us, to train us, to prepare us for a more developed state. Christ has manifested in His own person the wonderful grace of God that is to deal with us as with sons, to educate us unto holiness, and so to prepare us for the full possession of our heavenly heritage. We are the many sons who are to be brought to glory by the discipline of grace.

Grace Has a Discipline

So then, first of all, grace has a discipline. We generally think of the law when we talk about schoolmasters and discipline, but grace itself has a discipline and a wonderful training power, too. The manifestation of grace is preparing us for the manifestation of glory. What the law could not do, grace is able to do and is doing. The free favor of God instills new principles, suggests new thoughts, and creates in us love for God and hatred of that which is opposed to God by inspiring us with gratitude. Happy are they who attend the school of the grace of God!

This grace of God entering into us shows us what was evil even more clearly than the commandment does. We receive a vital, testing principle within, whereby we discern between good and evil. The grace of God provides us with instruction, but also with chastisement, as it is written, *"As many as I love, I rebuke and chasten"* (Revelation 3:19). As soon as we come under the conscious enjoyment of the free grace of God, we find it to be a holy rule, a fatherly government, a heavenly training. We do not find self-indulgence, much less licentiousness. On the contrary, the grace of God both restrains and constrains us. It makes us free to holiness and delivers us from the law of sin and death by *"the law of the Spirit of life in Christ Jesus"* (Romans 8:2).

Chosen Disciples of Grace

In addition to grace having its discipline, grace has its chosen disciples. You cannot help noticing that while the eleventh verse says, *"the grace of God that bringeth salvation hath appeared to all men,"* yet it is clear that this grace of God has not exercised its holy discipline upon all men. Therefore, the text changes its *"all men"* into *"us"* and *"we"* in the twelfth verse. Usually in Scripture when you find a generality, you soon find a particularity near it. This text follows that pattern: *"Teaching us that, denying ungodliness and worldly lusts, we should live soberly, righteously, and godly, in this present world."* Thus, grace has its own disciples.

Are you a disciple of the grace of God? Did you ever come and submit yourself to it? Have you learned to spell that word, "f–a–i–t–h"? Do you have childlike trust in Jesus? Have you learned to wash in the basin of atonement? Have you learned those holy exercises which are taught by the grace of God? Can you say that your salvation is of grace? Do you know the meaning of that text, *"By grace are ye saved through faith; and that not of yourselves: it is the gift of God"* (Ephesians 2:8)? If so, then you are His disciples, and the grace of God that has appeared so conspicuously has come to discipline you.

As the disciples of grace, endeavor to adore its doctrine. According to the previous verses, even a slave might do this. He might be an ornament to the grace of God. Let grace have such an effect upon your life and character that all may say, "See what grace can do! See how the grace of God produces holiness in believers!" All along I wish to be driving home the same point at which the apostle is aiming: we are to be holy because grace exercises a purifying discipline and because we are the disciples of that grace.

According to the apostle, the discipline of grace has three results: denying, living, and looking. You see the three words before you; the first is *"denying."* When a young man comes to college, he usually has much to unlearn. If his education has been neglected, a sort of instinctive ignorance covers his mind with briars and brambles. If he has gone to some faulty school where the teaching is flimsy, his tutor has first of all to extract out of him what he has been badly taught. The most difficult part of the training of young men is not to put the right thing into them, but to get the wrong thing out of them. A man proposes to teach a language in six months; in the end a great thing is accomplished if one of his pupils is able to forget all his nonsense in six years.

The Discipline of Denying

When the Holy Spirit comes into the heart, He finds that we know so much already of what it would have been good to leave unknown: we are self-conceited and puffed up; we have learned lessons of worldly wisdom and carnal policy. These we need to unlearn and deny. The Holy Spirit works this denying in us by the discipline of grace.

What do we have to deny? First, we have to deny ungodliness. This is a lesson that many of you have a great need to learn. Listen to men who are employed as manual laborers. "Oh," they say, "we have to work hard; we cannot think about

God or religion." This is ungodliness! The grace of God teaches us to deny this, and we come to loathe such atheism. Others who are striving in the world of commerce cry out such excuses as, "If you had as much business to look after as I have, you would have no time to think about your soul or another world. Trying to battle with the competition of the times leaves me no opportunity for prayer or Bible reading; I have enough to do with my schedules and ledger." This also is ungodliness! The grace of God leads us to deny this; we abhor such forgetfulness of God.

A great work of the Holy Spirit is to make a man godly, to make him think of God, to make him feel that this present life is not all, but to realize that there is a judgment to come, wherein he must *"give account of himself to God"* (Romans 14:12). God cannot be forgotten with impunity. If we treat Him as if He were nothing and leave Him out of our calculations for life, we will make a fatal mistake. O my friend, there is a God, and as surely as you live, you are accountable to Him. When the Spirit of God comes with the grace of the Gospel, He removes our ingrained ungodliness and causes us to deny it with joyful earnestness.

We next deny *"worldly lusts,"* the lusts of the present world or age, which I described to you just now as coming in between the two appearings. This present age is as full of evil lusts as that in which Paul wrote concerning the Cretans. *"All that is in the world, the lust of the flesh, and the lust of the eyes, and the pride of life"* (1 John 2:16) are yet with us. Wherever the grace of God comes effectually, it makes the person who lives loosely deny the desires of the flesh: it causes the man who lusted after gold to conquer his greediness; it brings the proud man away from his ambitions; it trains the idler to diligence; and it sobers the wanton mind which cared only for the frivolities of life. Not only do we leave these lusts, but we deny them. We have an abhorrence of those things in which we formerly placed our delight. Our cry is, *"What have I to do any more with idols?"* (Hosea 14:8). To the worldling we say, "These things may belong to you; but as for us, we cannot own them: *'Sin shall not have dominion over* [us]' (Romans 6:14). We are not of the world, and therefore its ways and fashions are none of ours."

The period in which we live should not have paramount influence over us, for our truest life is with Christ in eternity and *"our conversation is in heaven"* (Philippians 3:20). The grace of God has made us deny the prevailing philosophies, glories, maxims, and fashions of this present world. In the best sense we are nonconformists. We desire to be crucified to the world and the world to us. This was a great thing for grace to do among the degraded sensualist of Paul's day, and it is no less a glorious achievement in these times.

The Discipline of Living

But, beloved, you cannot be complete with a merely negative religion; you must have something positive. Thus, the next word is about living: *"We should live soberly, righteously, and godly, in this present world."* Observe, dear friends, that the Holy Spirit expects us to live in this present world, and therefore we are not to exclude ourselves from it. This age is the battlefield in which the soldier of Christ is to fight. Society is the place in which Christianity is to exhibit the grace of Christ. If some good sisters were to retire into a large house and live secluded from the world, they would be shirking their duty rather than fulfilling it. If all the good, true men were to form a select colony and do nothing else but pray and hear sermons, they would simply be refusing to serve God in His own appointed way. No, you have to live soberly, godly, and righteously in this world, such as it is at present. It is of no use for you to scheme to escape from it. You are bound to confront this torrent and withstand all its waves. If the grace of God is in you, that grace is meant to be displayed, not in a select and secluded retreat, but in this present world. You are to shine in the darkness like a light.

This lifestyle is described in a three-fold way. First, you are to live *"soberly,"* that is, for yourself. You are to live *"soberly"* in all your eating and your drinking and in the indulgence of all bodily appetites—that goes without saying. Drunkards and gluttons, fornicators and adulterers, cannot inherit the kingdom of God (1 Corinthians 6:9–10). You are to live soberly in all your thinking, all your speaking, all your acting. There is to be sobriety in all your worldly pursuits. You are to have yourself well in hand: you are to be self-restrained.

I know some brothers who are not often sober. I do not accuse them of being drunk with wine. Rather, they are mentally intoxicated: they have no reason, no moderation, no judgment. They are all spur and no rein. Right or wrong, they must have that which they have set their hearts upon. They never look around to take the full bearing of a matter. They never evaluate calmly, but with closed eyes they rush in like bulls. Alas, for these unsober people! They are not to be depended on; they are everything by turns and nothing for long. The man who is disciplined by the grace of God becomes thoughtful, considerate, self-contained. He is no longer tossed about by passion or swayed by prejudice.

There is only one insobriety into which I pray we may fall. Truth to say, it is the truest sobriety. Of this the Scripture says, *"Be not drunk with wine, wherein is excess; but be filled with the Spirit"* (Ephesians 5:18). When the Spirit of God takes full possession of us, then we are borne along by His sacred energy and are filled with a divine enthusiasm which needs no restraint. However, when we are exposed to all other influences, we must guard ourselves against yielding too completely, so that we may thus live *"soberly."*

As to his fellowmen, the believer is to live *"righteously."* I cannot understand any Christian who can do a dirty, dishonest thing in business. Craft, cunning, overreaching, misrepresentation, and deceit are no instruments for the hands of godly men. I am told that my principles are too angelic for business life, that a man cannot be a match for his fellowmen in trade if he is too Puritanical. Others are up to tricks, and he would be ruined if he could not trick them in return. O my dear believers, do not talk in this way. If you mean to go the way of the Devil, say so and take the consequences. However, if you profess to be servants of God, deny all partnership with unrighteousness. Dishonesty and falsehood are the opposites of godliness. A Christian man may be poor, but he must live righteously; he may lack sharpness, but he must not lack integrity. A Christian profession without uprightness is a lie. Grace must discipline us to righteous living.

We are told in the text that we are to live godly towards God. Every man who truly has the grace of God in him will think much of God and will *"seek...first the kingdom of God, and his righteousness"* (Matthew 6:33). God will enter into all his calculations, God's presence will be his joy, God's strength will be his confidence, God's providence will be his inheritance, God's glory will be the chief end of his being, and God's law the guide of his conversation. Now, if the grace of God that has appeared so plainly to all men has really come with its sacred discipline upon us, it is teaching us to live in this three-fold manner.

The Discipline of Looking

In addition, there is looking as well as living. One work of the grace of God is to cause us to be *"looking for that blessed hope and the glorious appearing of the great God and our Savior Jesus Christ."* What is that *"blessed hope"*? First, that when He comes, we will rise from the dead if we

133

have fallen asleep; and that, if we are alive and remain, we will be changed at His appearing. (See 1 Thessalonians 4:15–16; 1 Corinthians 15:51–53.) Our hope is that we will be approved of Him and will hear Him say, *"Well done, thou good and faithful servant"* (Matthew 25:21). This hope is not of debt, but of grace; although our Lord will give us a reward, it will not be according to the law of works.

"But we know that, when [Jesus] *shall appear, we shall be like him; for we shall see him as he is"* (1 John 3:2). When Jesus shines forth as the sun, *"then shall the righteous shine forth as the sun in the kingdom of their Father"* (Matthew 13:43). Our gain by godliness cannot be counted into the palm of a hand; rather, it lies in the glorious future. Yet, to one with faith, it is so near that at this moment I almost hear the chariot of the Coming One. The Lord is coming, and in His coming lies the great hope of the believer—his great stimulus to overcome evil, his main incentive to perfect holiness in the fear of the Lord. Oh, to be found blameless in the day of the manifestation of our Lord! May God grant us this! Do you see, beloved, how the discipline of the doctrine of grace runs toward separating us from sin and making us live unto God?

WORDS OF ENCOURAGEMENT

Finally, our text sets forth certain encouragements for us. I will only briefly hint at them even though the passage is rich beyond measure with hope for the future.

In this great battle for right and truth and holiness, what could we do, my friends, if we were left alone? Our first encouragement is that grace has come to our rescue. In the day when the Lord Jesus Christ appeared among men, He brought for us the grace of God to help us to overcome all iniquity. He that struggles now against inbred sin has the Holy Spirit within him to help him. He that goes forth to fight against evil in other men by preaching the Gospel has that same Holy Spirit going with the truth to make it *"like a fire...and like a hammer"* (Jeremiah 23:29). I would throw down my weapons and retreat from so hopeless a fight were it not that *"the LORD of hosts is with us; the God of Jacob is our refuge"* (Psalm 46:7). The grace of God that brings salvation from sin has flashed forth conspicuously like the lightning which is seen from one part of the heaven to the other, and our victory over darkness is insured. However hard the conflict with evil, it is not desperate. We may hope on and hope ever.

A certain warrior was discovered in prayer, and when his king sneered, he answered that he was pleading with his majesty's strongest ally. (I question whether God is the ally of anybody when he goes forth with gun and sword.) However, in using those *"weapons of our warfare* [which] *are not carnal, but mighty through God to the pulling down of strong holds"* (2 Corinthians 10:4), we may truly count on our noble Ally. Speak the truth, man, for God speaks with you! Work for

God, woman, for God *"worketh in you both to will and to do of his good pleasure"* (Philippians 2:13). The appearance of the grace of God in the person of Christ is encouragement enough to those who are under the most difficult circumstances and have to contend for righteousness against the deadliest odds. Grace has appeared; therefore, let us be of good courage!

His Promise to Return

A second encouragement is that another appearing is coming. He who bowed His head in weakness and died in the moment of victory is coming in all the glory of His endless life. Do not question it. The world is not going to darken into an eternal night; the morning comes as well as the night. Though sin and corruption abound and the love of many waxes cold, these are but the tokens of the near advent of Him who said that it would be so before His appearing. The right with the might and the might with the right will be: as surely as God lives, it must be so. We are not fighting a losing battle. The Lord must triumph.

If His suffering life and cruel death had been the only appearing, we might have feared. But it is not: it is but the first and the preparatory part of His manifestation. He comes! He comes! None can hinder His coming! Every moment brings Him nearer; nothing can delay His glory. When the hour strikes, He will appear in the majesty of God to put an end to the dominion of sin and bring in endless peace. Satan will be bruised under our feet shortly. *"Wherefore comfort one another with these words"* (1 Thessalonians 4:18), and then prepare for further battle. Sharpen your swords, and be ready for close fighting! Trust in God, and keep your powder dry. Ever this be our war cry, "He must reign." We look for *"the glorious appearing of the great God and our Saviour Jesus Christ."*

We Serve a Living Master

Another encouragement is that we serve a glorious Master. The Christ whom we follow is not a dead prophet like Mohammed. Truly we preach Christ crucified; but we also believe in Christ risen from the dead, in Christ gone up on high, in Christ soon to come a second time. He lived, and He lives as the great God and our Savior.

If you are indeed soldiers of such a Captain, throw fear to the winds. Can you be cowards when the Lord of Hosts leads you? Dare you tremble when at your head is the Wonderful, the Counselor, the mighty God, the everlasting Father, the Prince of Peace (Isaiah 9:6)? The trumpet is already at the lip of the archangel; who will not act like a man? The great drum that makes the universe to throb summons you to action.

> Stand up, stand up for Jesus,
> Ye soldiers of the cross;
> Lift high His royal banner;
> It must not suffer loss.

His cross is the old cross still, and none can overthrow it. Hallelujah to the name of Jesus!

Then come the tender thoughts with which I finish, the memories of what the Lord has done for us to make us holy: *"Who gave himself for us."* We have special redemption, redemption with a wondrous price: *"Who gave himself for us."* Put away that trumpet and that drum; take down the harp and gently touch its sweetest strings. Tell how the Lord Jesus loved us and gave Himself for us. Beloved, if nothing else can touch your hearts, this must: *"Ye are not your own, for ye are bought with a price"* (1 Corinthians 6:19–20).

Christ gave Himself for us with two objectives. The first is redemption, that He might redeem us from all iniquity, so that He might break the bonds of sin asunder and so that He might cast the cords of depravity far from us. He died—forget not that—died that your sins might die, died that every lust might be dragged into captivity under His chariot wheels. He gave Himself for you that you might give yourselves for Him.

Secondly, He died that He might purify us—purify us unto Himself. How clean we must be if we are to be clean unto Him. The holy Jesus will only commune with that which He has purified after the manner of His own nature, purified unto Himself. He has purified us to be wholly His. No human hand may use the golden cup; no human incense may burn in the consecrated censer. We are purified unto Himself, as the Hebrew would put it, to be His *cegullah*, His "unique possession." The translation *"peculiar people"* is unfortunate because the word *peculiar* has come to mean odd, strange, bizarre. The phrase really means that believers are Christ's own people, His choice and select portion. Saints are Christ's crown jewels; His box of diamonds; His very, very, very own. He carries His people as lambs in His bosom; He engraves their names on His heart. They are the inheritance to which He is the heir, and He values them more than all the universe beside. He would lose everything else sooner than lose one of them. He desires that you who are being disciplined by His grace should know that you are altogether His. You are Christ's. Each one of you is to know, "I do not belong to this world or even to myself; I belong only to Christ. I am set aside by Him for Himself only, and His I will be." The silver and the gold are His, and the cattle upon a thousand hills are His; but He makes small account of them. *"The LORD'S portion is his people"* (Deuteronomy 32:9).

Zealously Serving by Good Works

The apostle finishes by saying that we are to be a people *"zealous of good works."* I desire before God that all Christian men and women were disciplined by divine grace until they became zealous for good works! In holiness, zeal is sobriety. We are not only to approve of good works and speak for them, but we are to be red-hot for them. We are to be on fire for everything that is right and true. We must not be content to be quiet and inoffensive, but we need to be *"zealous of good works."* May the Lord's grace set us on fire in this way.

There is plenty of fuel in the church; what is lacking is fire. A great many people, all very respectable, are, in their sleepy way, doing as little as they can for any good cause. This will never do. We must wake up!

The quantity of ambulance work that Christ's soldiers have to do is overwhelming! One half of Christ's army has to carry the other half. May our fellow saints get off the sick list! Oh, that all of us were ardent, fervent, vigorous, and zealous! Come, Holy Spirit, and quicken us! We cannot go about to get this by our own efforts and energies, but God will work it by His grace. Grace given us in Christ is the fountainhead of all holy impulse. O heavenly grace, come like a flood at this time and bear us away!

May those of you who have never felt the grace of God be enabled to believe in the Lord Jesus Christ as to His first appearing! Then, trusting in His death upon the cross, you will learn to look for His Second Coming upon His white steed, and you will rejoice therein. Unto His great name be glory forever and ever! Amen.

Chapter Six

Preparation for the Coming of the Lord

And now, little children, abide in him; that, when he
shall appear, we may have confidence, and not be
ashamed before him at his coming.
—1 John 2:28

My first, most fervent desire is that my
readers would come to Christ. I stretch
myself to lift Him up just *"as Moses
lifted up the serpent in the wilderness"* (John 3:14),
and to bid men look to Him and live. There is no
salvation except by faith in the Lord Jesus Christ.
He said, *"Look unto me, and be ye saved, all the
ends of the earth: for I am God, and there is none
else"* (Isaiah 45:22).

When you have looked to Jesus, my next concern is that you may be found in Christ, the City of
Refuge. I long to speak of you as "people in Christ
Jesus." My beloved, you must be in living, loving,
lasting union with the Son of God, or else you are
not in a state of salvation. That which begins with
coming to Christ continues in your growing into
Him and receiving of His life, as the engrafted

branch is bound to the vine. You must be in Christ as the stone is in the building, as the member is in the body.

When I have good hope that my readers have come to Christ and are in Christ, a further concern springs up in my heart: that they may *"abide in him."* My longing is that, despite temptations to go away from Him, you may always remain at His feet; that, notwithstanding the evil of your nature, you may never betray your Master but may faithfully hold to Him. I would have you mindful of this precept: *"As ye have therefore received Christ Jesus the Lord, so walk ye in him"* (Colossians 2:6). Oh, that you may be rooted in Him, may be built up in Him, and may always be in union with Him! Then I may be able to present you to our Lord in the day of His appearing *"with exceeding great joy"* (Matthew 2:10).

I want to pay attention to this third burden of all those who minister for Christ. John said, *"Little children, abide in him."* How sweetly those words must have flowed from the lips and the pen of such a venerable saint! In this I think the beloved disciple echoed the Lord Jesus, who had told His disciples:

> [4] *Abide in me, and I in you. As the branch cannot bear fruit of itself, except it abide in the vine; no more can ye, except ye abide in me.*
>
> [7] *If ye abide in me, and my words abide in you, ye shall ask what ye will, and it shall be done unto you.*   (John 15:4, 7)

That word *abide* was a very favorite one with the Lord Jesus, and it became equally dear to that disciple whom Jesus loved. In our King James Version, the translators have interpreted it sometimes as "remain" and sometimes as "continue," but it was not very wise of them to have repeatedly shifted the rendering. It is one of the virtues of the Revised Version that it generally translates the same Greek word with the same English word. This may not be absolutely requisite, for a little variety may be tolerated, but it is eminently instructive since it allows us to see in our own language where the Holy Spirit used the same word. If the translation is correct in one case, we may naturally conclude it will not be incorrect in another. *Abide* was one of John's special words.

May the Lord help us to consider these blessed words! Better still, may He write them on our hearts, and may we fulfill their teaching!

First, notice what John exhorted them to do: *"abide in him."* Secondly, note how he addressed them: *"little children."* Finally, consider what motive he gave them: *"that, when he shall appear, we may have confidence, and not be ashamed before him at his coming."*

ABIDE IN CHRIST

First, then, observe what John was exhorting them to do: *"abide in him."* By this he meant one thing, but that thing is so comprehensive that we may better understand it by viewing it from many sides.

John meant fidelity to the truth taught by our Lord. We are sure he meant this, because a little previously he had said, *"If that which ye have heard from the beginning shall remain in you, ye also shall continue in the Son, and in the Father"* (1 John 2:24). Beloved, you have believed in the Lord Jesus Christ unto the salvation of your souls. You have trusted in Him as the Son of God, the appointed Mediator, and the effectual sacrifice for your sin. Your hope has come from a belief in Christ as God has borne witness to Him. Abide in the truth that you received from the beginning, for in your earliest days it wrought salvation in you. The foundation of your faith is not a changeable doctrine: you rest on a sure word of testimony. Truth is, in its very nature, fixed and unalterable. You know more about it than you did, but the truth itself is still the same and must be the same. Take care that you abide in it. You will find it difficult to do so, for there is an element of changeableness about yourself; this you must overcome by grace.

You will find many elements of seduction in the outside world. There are men whose business it is to shake the faith of others and thereby to gain a repute for cleverness and depth of thought. Some seem to think it an ambition worthy of a Christian to be always questioning, or, as Paul put it, to be *"ever learning, and never able to come to the knowledge of the truth"* (2 Timothy 3:7). Their chosen career is to throw doubt into minds that have been made blessed by a gracious certainty. Therefore, you will often be led to test your foundation, and at times you will tremble as you cling to it.

Pay attention, then, to this word from the mouth of your Lord: *"abide in him."* Keep to where you were as to the truth which you believe. That which has justified you will sanctify you. That which has, in a measure, sanctified you will yet perfect you. Make no change as to the eternal truths upon which you ground your hope. As a stone, you are built on the foundation; abide there. As a branch, you have been grafted into the stem; abide there. As a member, you are in the body; abide there. It is all over with you if you do not. Abide in that holy mold of doctrine into which you were at first delivered. Let no man deceive you with vain words, though there are many abroad in these days who, *"if it were possible,* [would] *deceive the very elect"* (Matthew 24:24). Abide in Jesus by letting His words abide in you. Believe what you have found to be the means of your quickening. Believe it with a greater intensity and a greater practicality. *"Cast not away therefore your confidence, which hath great recompense of reward"* (Hebrews 10:35).

Constancy of Trust

Next, John meant *"abide in him"* as to the loyalty of your trust. When you first enjoyed a hope, you rested upon Christ alone. I think I heard the first babbling of your infant faith when it said,

I'm a poor sinner and nothing at all,
But Jesus Christ is my all in all.

At first, you had no experience upon which you could rely and no inward graces upon which you could depend; you rested wholly upon Christ and His finished work. In no degree did you rest upon the works of the law, your own feelings, your own knowledge, or even your own resolves. Christ was all. Do you not remember how you used to tell others that the gospel precept was *"Only believe"* (Mark 5:36)? You cried to them, "Trust in Jesus. Get out of yourselves. Find all your needs provided for in Him."

Now, beloved, you have experience; thank God for it. Now you have the graces of the Spirit; thank God for them. Now you know the things of God by the teaching of the Holy Spirit; be grateful for that knowledge. However, do not fly in the face of your Savior now by putting your experience, your graces, or your knowledge, where He and He alone must be. Depend today as simply as you depended then. If you have some idea that you are hastening towards perfection, take care that you do not indulge a vain conceit about yourself. But, even if it is true, still do not mix your perfection with His perfection, or your advance in grace with the foundation that He has laid for you in His blood and righteousness. *"Abide in him."*

Jesus is the good ship into which you have entered so that He may bear you safe to the desired haven. Abide in the vessel. Neither venture to walk on the water, like Peter, nor think to swim by your own strength; instead, *"abide in him,"* and you will weather every storm. Only as you keep to your first simple confidence in the perfect work of the Lord Jesus can you have peace and salvation. As it is written, *"Thou wilt keep him in perfect peace, whose mind is stayed on thee: because he trusteth in thee"* (Isaiah 26:3).

Christ, Our Constant Object

Moreover, abide in the Lord Jesus Christ by making Him the constant object of your life. As you live by Christ, so live for Christ. Ever since you trusted in Christ's dying for you, you have felt that if He died for you, then you died in Him, and that henceforth your life might be consecrated to Him. You are not your own, but you are Christ's, and Christ's only. The first object of your being is to honor and serve Him who loved you and gave Himself for you (Galatians 2:20). You have not followed after wealth, honor, or self-pleasing, but you have followed Jesus. Take heed that you *"abide in him"* by continuing to serve Him.

> [15] *Love not the world, neither the things that are in the world. If any man love the world, the love of the Father is not in him.*
> [16] *For all that is in the world, the lust of the flesh, and the lust of the eyes, and the pride of life, is not of the Father, but is of the world.*
> [17] *And the world passeth away, and the lust thereof: but he that doeth the will of God abideth for ever.* (1 John 2:15–17)

You may wisely continue where you are, for you have chosen the right pursuit, and you have entered upon the right road. The crown that glitters in your eye at the end of the race is worthy of all your running. You could not have a nobler motivating power than the constraining love of Christ. To live for Christ is the highest lifestyle; continue in it more and more. If the Lord changes your circumstances, still live for Christ. If you go up, take Christ up with you. If you go down, Christ will go down with you. If you are in health, live for Christ earnestly. If you are bound to a sickbed, live for Christ patiently. Go about your business, and sing for Jesus; or if He bids you stay at home and cough away your life, then do so for Jesus. Just let everything be for Him. For you, *excelsior* means higher consecration, more heavenly living.

Persevering in Obedience

Surely, we should also understand that, by abiding in Him, we are to persevere in our obedience to our Lord. The next verse is, *"If ye know that he is righteous, ye know that every one that doeth righteousness is born of him"* (v. 29). Whatever your Lord bids you to do, continue to do. Call no man "Master," but in all things submit your thoughts, your words, and your acts to the rule of the Lord Jesus. Obey Him by whose obedience you are justified. Be precise and prompt in your execution of His commands. If others consider you morbidly conscientious, do not heed their opinions, but *"abide in him."* The Master's rule is always binding on all His disciples, and they depart from Him in heart when they stray from His rule.

Obedience to the precept is as much included in our honor of Christ as faith in the doctrine. If you have been upright in your dealings, be upright now; be accurate to the penny in every payment. If you have been loving and generous, be loving and generous now; your Lord's law is love. If you have closely imitated the Lord Jesus, go on to copy Him still more precisely. Seek no new model; pray that the Holy Spirit would work the same thing in you. As a soldier, your Captain's word is law.

> Yours is not to reason why,
> Yours is but to do and die.

"Abide in him." I know you might be rich by doing that un-Christlike act: scorn to win wealth in such a way. I know you may involve yourself in persecution if you follow your Lord closely. Accept such persecution gladly, and rejoice in it for His name's sake. I know that a great many would say that for charity's sake you must make compromises by being in conformity with evil doctrines and worldly practices, but you know better. It is yours to follow the Lamb wherever He goes. This is what His beloved apostle meant when he said, *"Abide in him."*

Vitally United with Christ

However, I have not completed the full description yet. I fear I am not able to do so by reason of my shallow knowledge and forgetfulness.

Continue in virtual union with your Lord. All the life you have is life derived from Him; seek no other. You are not a Christian unless Jesus is the Christ of God to you. You are not alive unto God unless you are one with the risen Lord. You are not saved unless He is your Savior, nor righteous unless He is your righteousness. You have not a single pulse of heavenly desire nor a breath of divine life in you except what was first given you from Him and is daily given to you by Him. Abide in this vital union. Do not try to lead an independent life. *"Abide in him"* from day to day in complete dependence upon the life that is stored up in Him on your behalf.

Be Directed by Him

Let your life *"abide in him"* in the sense of being directed by Him. The head directs all the members. The order that lifts the hand, spreads the palm, closes the fist, or lowers the arm comes from the brain, which is the headquarters of the soul. Abide in your Lord by implicitly owning His headship. Let every regulation of your life come from Him who is the head (Ephesians 4:15), and let it be obeyed as naturally as the desires of the mind coming from the brain are obeyed by every part of the body.

There is no war between the hand and the foot because they abide in the head. Thus, they are ruled without force and guided without violence. If the leg were to set up an independent authority over itself instead of obeying the head, what strange walking we should see! Have you ever met with afflicted people in whom the nerves have lost their function and the muscles seem to jerk at random, throwing out a leg or an arm without reason? Such movements are painful to see, and we know that such a man is diseased. Do not desire to be without law to Christ. *"Let this mind be in you, which was also in Christ Jesus"* (Philippians 2:5). In that respect, *"abide in him."*

Christ, Our Element of Life

"Abide in him" as the element of your life. Let Him encompass you as the air surrounds you on all sides. As a fish, whether it be the tiniest sprat or the biggest whale, abides in the sea, so you abide in Christ. The fish does not seek the sky or the shore; it could not live out of the element of water. Just so, I beseech you, do not seek to live in the world and in its sins, because as a Christian you cannot live there—Christ is your life. There is room enough for you in the Lord Jesus Christ because He is the infinite God. Do not go outside of Him for anything. Seek not pleasure or treasure outside of Christ, for such pleasure or treasure would be ruinous. Have neither want, nor will, nor wish, beyond your Lord. Let Him draw a line around you, and abide within that circle.

At Home in Him

"Abide in him" in the sense of being at home in Him. What a world of meaning I intend by that

phrase, "being at home in Christ." Yet, this is the sense of the word, *"abide in him."* Recently, I spoke to a friend who had bought a pleasant house with a large garden. He told me, "I now feel as if I have a home. I had lived in London for years and had moved from one house to another with as little regret as a man feels in changing a bus. But I have always longed for the home feeling that was about my father's house in the country. Why, there we loved the cozy rooms, the lookouts from the little windows, and the corner cupboards in the kitchen. As for the garden and the field, they yielded us constant delight, for there was that bush in the garden where the robin had built her nest and the tree with the blackbird's nest. We knew where the pike stayed in the pool, where the tortoise had buried itself for the winter, and where the first primroses would be found in the spring. A vast difference exists between a house and a home." That is what John meant with regard to Christ: we are not merely to call on Him, but to *"abide in him."*

Do not go to Jesus one day and to the world the following day. Do not be a day-to-day lodger with Him, but *"abide in him."* My friend spoke of changing from one bus to another, and I fear that some change from Christ to the world when the day changes from Sunday to Monday; but it should not be so.

Say with Moses, *"LORD, thou hast been our dwelling place in all generations"* (Psalm 90:1). Lord, Your cross is the roof-timber of the family of love. Within the thorn-hedge of Your suffering love, our whole estate is surrounded. Your name is named on our abiding place. We are not tenants with a lease to You, but we have a freehold in You. Lord Jesus, we are at home nowhere but in You; in You we abide. Wherever else we lodge, we have in due time to shift quarters. Whatever else we have, we lose it or leave it; but You are the same, and You change not. We can truly say and sing:

> Here would I make a settled rent
> While others go and come:
> No more a stranger or a guest,
> But like a child at home.

What a comfort to have our Lord Himself to be our chosen dwelling place in time and in eternity!

Now, I think I have come nearer to the full sense of the text. *"Abide in him"* means hold fast to Him, live in Him, let all your noblest powers be drawn forth in connection with Him as a man at home replenishes his strength. Feel at ease in fellowship with Him. Say, *"Return unto thy rest, O my soul; for the LORD hath dealt bountifully with thee"* (Psalm 116:7).

Remain with Him

Why did John urge us to abide in Christ? Is there any likelihood of our going away from Him? Yes, for in this very chapter, John mentioned apostates who had degenerated from disciples into antichrists. Of them he said, *"They went out from us, but they were not of us; for if they had been of us, they would no doubt have continued with us"*

(1 John 2:19). *"Abide in him,"* then, and do not turn aside unto crooked ways as many professing Christians have done. The Savior once asked His apostles, *"Will ye also go away?"* (John 6:67), and they answered Him with that other question, *"Lord, to whom shall we go? thou hast the words of eternal life"* (John 6:68). I hope your heart is so conscious that He has the words of eternal life that you could not dream of going elsewhere.

"But surely it is implied in these warnings that saints do leave their Lord and perish?" I answer, "No." Carefully observe the provision which is made against that fatality—provision to enable us to carry out the precept of the text. Just look at the verse which immediately precedes our text. What do you see? *"Ye shall abide in him"* (1 John 2:27). Then, the passage continues, *"And now, little children, abide in him."* There is a promise made to those who are in Christ that they *"shall abide in him."*

However, that promise does not render the precept unnecessary, for the Lord deals with us as with reasonable beings, not as with sticks and stones. He secures the fulfillment of His own promise that we *"shall abide in him"* by impressing upon our hearts His sacred precept, whereby He bids us to *"abide in him."* The force He uses to effect His purpose is instruction, heart-winning, and persuading. We abide in Christ, not by a physical law, as a mass of iron abides on the earth, but by a mental and spiritual law, by which the greatness of divine love and goodness holds us fast to the Lord. You have the guarantee that you will abide in Christ in the covenant agreement, *"I will put my fear in their hearts, that they shall not depart from me"* (Jeremiah 32:40). What a blessed promise that is! You are to take care that you abide in Christ as much as if all depended upon yourself; and yet, you can look to the promise of the covenant and see that the real reason for your abiding in Christ lies in the operation of His unchanging love and grace.

The Holy Spirit, Our Abiding Helper

Moreover, beloved, if you are in Christ Jesus, you have the Holy Spirit given to you to enable you to *"abide in him."* Read the entire verse that precedes our text: *"But the anointing which ye have received of him abideth in you, and ye need not that any man teach you: but as the same anointing teacheth you of all things, and is truth, and is no lie, and even as it hath taught you, ye shall abide in him"* (1 John 2:27). The Holy Spirit brings the truth home to your heart with savor and unction, endearing it to your innermost soul. The truth has so saturated you through the anointing that you cannot give it up. Has not your Lord said, *"The water that I shall give him shall be in him a well of water springing up into everlasting life"* (John 4:14)?

Thus, you see that what is commanded in one Scripture is promised and provided for in another. God's commands are enabling to His people. As He bids you to abide in Him, He causes you to abide in Him to His praise and glory by that very bidding.

Secondly, notice how John addresses these believers. He says, *"And now, little children."* This indicates the apostle's love for them. John lived to a great age. Tradition has it that they used to carry him into the assembly, and, when he could do nothing else, he would lift his hand and simply say, *"Little children...love one another"* (1 John 4:4, 7). Here, to show his tender concern for those to whom he wrote, he called them *"little children."* He could not wish them a greater blessing out of the depth of his heart's affection than that they should faithfully abide in Christ.

In Right Relationship with the Lord

By the address of *"little children,"* John reminded them of their near and dear relationship to their Father in heaven. You are the children of God, but as yet you are little ones; therefore, do not leave your Father's house or run away from your Elder Brother's love. Because you are little children, you are not of traveling years; therefore, stay at home and abide in your Lord.

Does he not also hint at their feebleness? Even if you were grown and strong, you would not be wise to gather all together and wander away into the far country; but since you are so young, so dependent, so feeble, it is essential that you *"abide in him."* Would a babe forsake his mother? What can you do apart from God? Is He not your life, your all?

Does not the apostle also gently allude to their fickleness? You are very changeable, like little babes. You are apt to be hot and cold in half an hour. You are this and that, and fifty other things, in the course of one revolving moon. But, little children as you are, be faithful to one point—abide in your Savior. Change not towards your Redeemer. Stretch out your hands, clasp Him, and cry,

> My Jesus, I love Thee,
>   I know Thou art mine,
> For Thee all the follies
>   Of sin I resign.

Surrender yourself to Him by an everlasting covenant never to be canceled. Be His forever and ever.

Daily Dependence

Did not this remind them of their daily dependence upon the Lord's care, just as little children depend on their parents? Beloved, the Lord has to nurse you. He feeds you with the unadulterated milk of the Word. He comforts you as a mother does her child. He carries you in His bosom. He bears you all your days. Your new life is as yet weak and struggling; do not carry it into the cold atmosphere of distance from Jesus. *"Little children,"* since you derive all from Jesus, *"abide in him."* To go elsewhere will be to wander into a howling wilderness. The world is empty; only Christ has fullness. Away from Jesus, you will be as a child deserted by its mother, left to pine and starve, or as a little lamb on the hillside without a shepherd, tracked by the wolf, whose teeth will soon extract its heart's blood. Abide, child, with your mother! Abide, lamb, with your Shepherd!

All Believers Are Included

We may all fit John's description at this time. The beloved John speaks to us as to little children, for none of us are much more. We are not such wonderfully knowing people as are certain of our neighbors. We are not such learned scientists or astute minds as they are. Neither have we their marvelous moral consciousness, which is superior to inspiration itself. Therefore, we are bound by our very feebleness to venture less than they do. Let the men of the world choose what paths they will; we feel bound to abide in Christ because we know no other place of safety. They may push off into the sea of speculation; our smaller boats must hug the shore of certainty. To us, however, it is no small comfort that the Lord has revealed to babes the things which are hidden from the wise and prudent (Matthew 11:25). Those who become as little children enter into the kingdom of heaven.

Cling to the Lord Jesus in your feebleness, in your fickleness, in your nothingness. Abidingly take Him to be everything to you. *"The conies are but a feeble folk, yet make they their houses in the rocks"* (Proverbs 30:26); follow their example, *"little children."* Abide in the rifts of the Rock of Ages, and let nothing tempt you to quit your stronghold. You are no lion, able to fight your foes and deliver yourself by brute strength; you are only a little cony, and you will be wise to hide rather than fight. *"Little children, abide in him."*

RIGHT MOTIVES

I now come to my last point, which is most important because it is the steam that drives the engine. We will consider what motivation John gave us for this pleasant, necessary duty of abiding in Christ.

Kindly look at the text, for there is in it a little word to be noticed. The apostle exhorted us by a motive in which he took his share. Let me read it: *"Now, little children, abide in him; that, when he shall appear,* [you] *may have confidence."* No, no. Look at that little word. It actually says, *"that...we may have confidence."* The beloved John needed to have confidence at the appearing of the Lord—confidence fetched from the same source as that to which he directed his little children. They must abide in Christ so that they might have confidence, and the dearest of the apostles must practice the same abiding. How wisely, and yet how sweetly, he put himself on our level in this matter!

Drawn from Jesus

Notice, further, that the motive is one drawn from Jesus. John did not drive believers with the lash of the law, but he drew them with the cords of love (Hosea 11:4). I never like to see God's children whipped with rods gathered from the thorny sides of Sinai. We have not come to Mount Sinai but to Mount Zion. When a man tries to pommel me to my duty by the law, I kick like a bullock unaccustomed to the yoke. Rightly so should I, because *"we are not under the law, but under grace"* (Romans 6:15). The motive which sways a freeborn heir of heaven is fetched from grace, not from law; from Jesus, not from Moses. Christ is our example and our motive also. Blessed be His name!

Two Perspectives of Christ's Coming

The motive is drawn from our Lord's expected advent. Notice how John expressed it. He used two phrases for this same thing: *"when he shall appear"* and *"at his coming."* The Second Advent may be viewed from two perspectives: first, as the appearing of one who is here already but is hidden, and, secondly, as the coming of one who is absent. In the first sense, we know that our Lord Jesus Christ abides in His church, according to His word, *"Lo, I am with you alway, even unto the end of the world"* (Matthew 28:20). Yet, though spiritually present, He is unseen. All of a sudden, our Lord will be *"manifested,"* as the Revised Version (RV) translates it in 1 John 2:28. The spiritual and secret presence of Christ will become a visible and manifest presence in the day of His appearing.

John also used the term, *"at his coming,"* or "His presence." This is the same thing from another point of view. In a certain evident sense, our Lord is absent: *"He is not here: for he is risen, as he said"* (Matthew 28:6). He has gone His way unto the Father. In that respect He will *"appear the second time without sin unto salvation"* (Hebrews 9:28). *"This same Jesus, which is taken up from you into heaven, shall so come in like manner as ye have seen him go into heaven"* (Acts 1:11). There is thus a difference of perspective between the descriptions of the Second Advent as "His appearing" and "His coming." John pleaded the glorious manifestation of our Lord under both of these views as a reason for abiding in Him.

Confidence, the Reward of Abiding

As to our Lord's appearing, John would have us abide in Christ so that we may have confidence when He appears. Confidence at His appearing is the high reward of constant abiding in Christ. The apostle keeps Christ's appearing most prominent as a motivation. A thousand things are to happen at our Lord's appearing, but John did not mention one of them. He did not hold it up as a thing to be desired that we may have confidence amid the wreck of matter and the crash of worlds; when the stars will fall like autumn leaves; when the sun will be turned into darkness and the moon into blood; when the graves will be opened and the dead rise; when the heavens, being on fire, will be dissolved and the elements will melt with fervent heat; or when the earth and the works therein will also be burned up. Those will be ominous times, days of terror and dismay. However, it is none of these that he referred to particularly, for he regarded all these events as swallowed up in the one great fact of *"the glorious appearing of the great God and our Saviour Jesus Christ"* (Titus 2:13).

His desire was that we may have confidence if Christ appears suddenly. What did John mean by having confidence *"when he shall appear"*? Just this: if you abide in Him when you do not see Him, you will be very bold should He suddenly reveal Himself. Before He appears, you have dwelt in Him, and He has dwelt in you; what fear could His appearing cause you? Your faith has so realized Him that, if suddenly He were to appear to your senses, it would be no surprise to you and would assuredly cause you joy rather than dismay. You would feel that, at last, you could enjoy what you had for so long expected, and you could see somewhat more closely your Friend with whom you had long been familiar. I trust, beloved, that some of us live in such a style that if our Lord were to appear suddenly, it would cause no alarm to us. We have believed Him to be present, though unseen, and it will not affect our conduct when He steps from behind the curtain and stands in the open light.

If the Lord Jesus were now to stand next to us, we should remember that we had His presence before and had lived in it, and now we should only be more assured of that which we before knew by faith. We should behold our Lord with confidence, freedom, assurance, and delight, feeling perfectly at home with Him. The believer who abides in his Lord would only be a little startled by His sudden appearing. If he is serving his Lord now, he would go on serving Him. He loves Him now, and he would go on loving Him. As he has a clearer view of Christ, he would only feel a more intense consecration to Him.

The Greek word *parrhesia,* translated here as *"confidence,"* means freedom of speech or outspokenness. If our divine Lord were to appear momentarily, we should not lose our speech through fear but should welcome Him with glad acclaim. To desert our Lord would rob us of that ease of mind which is implied by free speech, but to cling to Him will secure us confidence.

We now speak to Him in secret, and He speaks back to us. We will not cease to speak in tones of reverent love when He appears. I have preached concerning my Lord, though He is not seen, the truths which I will not blush to own before His face. If my Lord and Master were, at this instant, to appear in His glory, I would dare with confidence hand to Him the volumes of my sermons as proof that I have not departed from His truth but have heartily continued in Him. I ought to improve in many things, but I could not improve upon the Gospel that I have preached. I am prepared to live by it, to die by it, or to meet my Lord upon it if He should this day appear.

O beloved, if you are in Christ, see to it that you so *"abide in him"* that, should He suddenly appear, you would behold Him with confidence. If we abide in Christ and He were to unveil His majestic face, we might be overcome with rapture; but our confidence in Him would grow stronger, our freedom with Him would be even more enlarged, and our joy in Him would be made perfect. Has He not prayed for us that we may be with

Him and behold His glory (John 17:24)? Can we be afraid of the answer to His loving prayer? If you abide in Christ, the manifestation of Christ will be your manifestation, which will be a matter of delight and not of fear.

Beloved, if you do not *"abide in him,"* you will have no confidence. If I were to compromise the truth, and then my Lord were to appear, could I meet Him with confidence? If, to preserve my reputation or to be thought liberal-minded, I played fast and loose with the Gospel, how could I see my Lord's face with confidence? If any of you have failed to serve your Master, if you have preferred gain to godliness and pleasure to holiness, if He were suddenly to shine forth in His glory, what confidence could you have in meeting Him?

Not Ashamed at His Return

One day a godly man was asked, "If the Lord were now to appear, how would you feel?" He replied, "My brother, I should not be afraid; but I think I would be ashamed." He meant that he was not afraid of condemnation, but he blushed to think how little he had served his Lord. In his case it was genuine humility. I pray that you not only get beyond being afraid, but that the Lord may make you so to *"abide in him"* that you would *"not be ashamed before him at his coming."*

Another aspect of *"not be*[ing] *ashamed before him at his coming"* is that, having regarded Him as being absent, you should not have so lived that you would be ashamed of your past if He suddenly appeared in person. What must it be like to be driven away from His presence with shame into everlasting contempt? The text may have such an implication.

What have you been doing while He has been absent? This is a question for a servant to answer at his Lord's arrival. You are left in His house to take care of it while He is in the far-off country. If you have been beating His servants and eating and drinking with the drunken, you will be greatly ashamed when He returns. His coming will be in itself a judgment. *"Who may abide the day of his coming? and who shall stand when he appeareth?"* (Malachi 3:2). Blessed is that man who, with all his faults, has been so sanctified by grace that he will not be ashamed at his Lord's coming. Who is that man? It is the man who has learned to abide in Christ.

Prepare Yourself

What is the way to prepare for Christ's coming? By the study of the prophecies? Yes, if you are sufficiently instructed to be able to understand them. "To be prepared for the Lord's coming," some enthusiasts might say, "should I not spend a month in retirement and remove myself from this wicked world?" You may, if you like, and especially you will do so if you are lazy. However, the one scriptural prescription for preparing for His coming is to *"abide in him."* If you abide in the faith of Him, holding His truth, following His example, and making Him your dwelling place, then your

Lord may come at any hour, and you will welcome Him. The cloud, the Great White Throne, the blast of trumpets, the angelic attendants of the last judicial court, the trembling of creation, and the rolling up of the universe as worn-out apparel will have no alarms for you because you will not be ashamed at His coming.

Always Be Ready

The date of Christ's return is concealed. (See Matthew 24:36.) No man can tell when He will come. Watch for Him, and be always ready, so that you may not be ashamed at His Advent. Should a Christian go into worldly assemblies and amusements? Would he not be ashamed should his Lord come and find him among the enemies of the cross? I dare not go where I would be ashamed to be found should my Lord come suddenly. Should a Christian man ever be in a rage? Suppose his Lord should come right then and there; would the man not be ashamed at His coming? Another person says about an offender, "I will never forgive her; she will never darken my doors again." Would not that one be ashamed if the Lord Jesus came and found her unforgiving? Oh, may we *"abide in him"* and never be in such a state that His coming would be unwelcome to us!

Beloved, so live daily in duty and in devotion that your Lord's coming would be timely. Go about your business and *"abide in him."* Then His coming will be a glorious delight to you. We are never in a better state for seeing our Master than when we are faithfully doing His work. There is no need for a pious smartening up. He who abides in Christ always wears garments of glory and beauty. He may go with his Lord into the wedding whenever the midnight cry is heard. *"Abide in him,"* and then none can make you ashamed. *"Who shall lay any thing to the charge of God's elect?"* (Romans 8:33).

He will come. Behold, He is coming even now. Do you not hear the sounding of His chariot wheels? He may arrive before the sun goes down. *"Therefore be ye also ready: for in such an hour as ye think not the Son of man cometh"* (Matthew 24:44). When the world is eating and drinking, marrying and giving in marriage, He will bring destruction upon the ungodly. Be so engaged, day by day, that you will not be taken unawares.

What it will be to be caught up together with the saints in the clouds, to meet the Lord in the air! What it will be to see Him come in the glory of the Father, and all His holy angels with Him! What it will be to see Him reign upon the earth, with His ancients, gloriously! Can you imagine the millennial splendor, the age of gold, the serene days of peace? As for the judgment of the world, *"Do ye not know that the saints shall judge the world...*[and] *angels?"* (1 Corinthians 6:2–3). We will appear as assessors with Christ, and *"the God of peace shall bruise Satan under* [our] *feet"* (Romans 16:20).

Glory awaits us, and nothing but glory, if we abide in Christ. Therefore, keep your garments unspotted, your loins girded, your lamps trimmed, your lights burning, and you yourselves as men that look for your Lord, in order that, when He comes, you may have confidence and not shame.

May the Holy Spirit, without whom this cannot happen, be freely given to us this day, in order that we may abide in the Lord! And you who have never trusted in Christ for salvation, may you come to Him and then *"abide in him"* from this good hour! To His name be glory! Amen.

Chapter Seven

Watching for Christ's Coming

Blessed are those servants, whom the lord when he
cometh shall find watching: verily I say unto you, that
he shall gird himself, and make them to sit down to
meat, and will come forth and serve them.
And if he shall come in the second watch, or come
in the third watch, and find them so,
blessed are those servants.
—Luke 12:37–38

S ince I am about to address another aspect of
Christ's Second Coming, I trust that you,
dear reader, are attuned to the subject now
and that you will not have to make any very great
exertion of mind to plunge into midstream and be
carried away with the full current of thought concerning our Savior's Second Advent.

This is a very appropriate subject when we
consider the Lord's Table because the Lord's Supper not only looks backward and is a memorial of
His agony, but it also looks forward and is an an-
ticipation of His glory. Paul wrote to the church at
Corinth, *"For as often as ye eat this bread, and*

drink this cup, ye do show the Lord's death till he come" (1 Corinthians 11:26). By looking forward in a right state of heart to that Second Coming of Christ, which is the joy of His church, you will also be in a right state of heart for coming to the communion table. May the Holy Spirit make it to be so!

According to our Lord's example, the posture at the communion table was not that of kneeling, but of reclining. The easiest position that you can assume is the most fitting for the Lord's Supper. Yet, remember that the Supper was no sooner finished than, *"when they had sung an hymn, they went out into the mount of Olives"* (Mark 14:26), to the agonies of Gethsemane.

It often seems to me as if now, after finding rest at the table by feeding upon Christ (whose real presence we have with us not in a physical way, but in a spiritual sense), that we could sing a hymn and then go out to meet our Lord at His Second Coming. We would not be going to the Mount of Olives to see Him in a bloody sweat, but to hear that word of the angel, *"This same Jesus, which is taken up from you into heaven, shall so come in like manner as ye have seen him go into heaven"* (Acts 1:11). I do not think we ought to feel at all surprised if we were to go out from the table of fellowship the next time we participate and meet our Lord at once.

We should be always waiting for His appearing, ever expecting Him, not knowing at what hour the Master of the house will come (Mark 13:35). The world does not expect Him; it goes on with its eating and drinking, its marrying and giving in marriage (Matthew 24:38–39). However, His own family should expect Him. When He will return, I trust that He will not find the door shut against Him, but that we will be ready to open to our Lord immediately when He knocks. That is the object of these few words, to stir you up to be ever watching for Christ's Second Coming.

The Lord Will Return

First, the Lord will come again. He who has come once is to come again; He will come a second time. We can be assured that the Lord will come again because He has promised to return. We have His own word for it. That is our first reason for expecting Him. Among the last of the words that He spoke to His servant John are these: *"Surely I come quickly"* (Revelation 22:20). You may read it, "I am coming quickly. I am even now upon the road. I am traveling as fast as wisdom allows. I am always coming, and coming quickly." Our Lord has promised to come, and to come in person.

Some try to explain the Second Coming as though it refers to the time when a believer dies. You may, if you like, consider that Christ comes to His saints in death. In a certain sense, He does; but that sense will never bear out the full meaning of the teaching of the Second Advent with which the Scripture is full. Rather, *"the Lord himself shall descend from heaven with a shout, with the voice of the archangel, and with the trump of God"* (1 Thessalonians 4:16). He who went up to heaven will come down from heaven, and *"He shall stand at the latter day upon the earth"* (Job 19:25). Every redeemed soul can say with Job, *"Though after my skin worms destroy this body, yet in my flesh shall I see God: Whom I shall see for myself, and mine eyes shall behold, and not another"* (Job 19:26–27). Christ will as certainly be here again in glory as He once was here in shame, for He has promised to return.

Redemption Requires Christ's Return

Moreover, the great scheme of redemption requires Christ's return. It is a part of the scheme that, as He came once as a sin-offering, He should *"appear the second time without sin unto salvation"* (Hebrews 9:28); that is, as He came once to redeem, He should come a second time to claim the inheritance that He has so dearly bought. He came once so that His heel might be bruised; He will come again to break the serpent's head and to dash His enemies in pieces as potters' vessels with a rod of iron. He came once to wear the crown of thorns; He must come again to wear the diadem of universal dominion. He comes to the marriage supper; He comes to gather His saints together; He comes to glorify them with Himself on this same earth where once He and they were *"despised and rejected of men"* (Isaiah 53:3).

Be sure of this: the whole drama of redemption cannot be perfected without this last act of the coming of the King. The complete history of *Paradise Regained* requires that the New Jerusalem should come down from God out of heaven, prepared as a bride adorned for her husband. It also requires that the heavenly Bridegroom should come riding forth on His white horse, conquering and to conquer, King of Kings and Lord of Lords, amid the everlasting hallelujahs of saints and angels. It must be so. The man of Nazareth will come again. None will spit in His face then, but every knee will bow before Him. The Crucified will come again, and although the nail prints will still be visible, no nails will then fasten His dear hands to the tree. Instead, He will grasp the scepter of universal sovereignty, and He will reign forever and ever. Hallelujah!

In His Own Time

When will He come? Ah, that is the question, the question of questions! He will come in His own time. He will come in due time.

Calling upon me, a brother minister said, as we sat together, "I would like to ask you a lot of questions about the future."

"Oh, well!" I replied, "I cannot answer you, for I know no more about it than you do."

"But," said he, "what about the Lord's Second Advent? Will there not be the Millennium first?"

I said, "I cannot tell with certainty whether the Millennium will be first, but this I know: the Scripture has left the whole matter with an intentional indistinctness, in order that we may be always expecting Christ to come and that we may be watching for His coming at any and every hour. I think that the Millennium will commence after His coming, and not before it. I cannot imagine the kingdom with the King absent. It seems to me to be an essential part of the millennial glory that the King would then be revealed. At the same time, I am not going to lay down anything definite upon that point. He may not come for a thousand years; He may come tonight. The teaching of Scripture is: *'In such an hour as ye think not the Son of man cometh'* (Matthew 24:44). It is clear that if it were revealed that a thousand years must elapse before He would return, we might very well go to sleep for the entire time because we would have no reason to expect that He would come when Scripture told us He would not."

"Well," answered my friend, "but when Christ comes, that will be the general judgment, will it not?" I then quoted these texts: *"The dead in Christ shall rise first"* (1 Thessalonians 4:16), and, *"But the rest of the dead lived not again until the thousand years were finished. This is the first resurrection"* (Revelation 20:5).

I replied, "There is a resurrection from among the dead to which the apostle Paul labored to attain (Philippians 3:11). We will all rise, but the righteous will rise a thousand years before the ungodly. There is to be that interval of time between the one and the other; whether that is the millennial glory or not, I will not say, although I think it is. But, this is the main point: the Lord will come. We know not when we are to expect His coming. We are not to lay down, as absolutely fixed, any definite prediction or circumstance that would allow us to go to sleep until that prediction was fulfilled or that circumstance was apparent."

"Will not the Jews be converted to Christ and restored to their land?" inquired my friend.

I responded, "Yes, I think so. *'They shall look upon* [him] *whom they have pierced, and they shall mourn for him, as one mourneth for his only son'* (Zechariah 12:10); God will give them the kingdom and the glory, for they are His people, whom He has not forever cast away (Romans 11:1–2). The Jews, who are the natural olive branches, will yet be grafted into their own olive tree again (see Romans 11:23–24), and then will be the fullness of the Gentiles."

"Will that be before Christ comes, or after?" asked my friend.

I answered, "I think it will be after He comes; but whether it is or not, I am not going to commit to any definite opinion on the subject."

I admonish you, my dear friends, to read and search the Scriptures for yourselves.

Still, this one thing stands first and is the only thing that I will insist upon now: the Lord will come. He may come now; He may come tomorrow; He may come in the first watch of the night or the second, or He may wait until the morning watch. Whenever He is coming again, the one word that He gives to you all is, "Watch! Watch!" Thus, whenever He does come, you may be ready to open to Him and to say, in the language of the hymn:

Hallelujah! Welcome,
Welcome, Judge divine!

So far, I know that we are scriptural and, therefore, perfectly safe in our statements about the Lord's Second Advent.

Ideas of Delay Can Be Harmful

Friends, I would be earnest on this point: the notion of the delay of Christ's coming is always harmful, however you arrive at it, whether it be by studying prophecy or in any other way. If you come to be of the opinion of the servant mentioned in the following text, you are wrong:

> [45] *But and if that servant say in his heart, My lord delayeth his coming; and shall begin to beat the menservants and maidens, and to eat and drink, and to be drunken;*
> [46] *The lord of that servant will come in a day when he looketh not for him, and at an hour when he is not aware, and will cut him in sunder, and will appoint him his portion with the unbelievers.* (Luke 12:45–46)

Do not, therefore, get the idea that the Lord delays His coming, and that He will not or cannot come as yet. Far better would it be for you to stand on tiptoe in expectation and to be rather disappointed to think that He does not come. I do not wish you to be shaken in mind so as to act fanatically or foolishly, as certain people did in America, when they went out into the woods with ascension dresses on, so as to go straight up all of a sudden. Fall into none of those absurd ideas that have led people to leave a chair vacant at the table or to set an empty plate because the Lord might come and want it. Try to avoid all other superstitious nonsense. To stand stargazing at the prophecies with your mouth wide open is just the wrong thing to do. Far better will it be to go on working for your Lord, getting yourself and your service ready for His appearing and cheering yourself, all the while telling yourself this: "While I am at work, my Master may come. Before I get weary, my Master may return. While others are mocking at me, my Master may appear. Whether they mock or applaud is nothing to me. I live before the great Taskmaster's eye and do my service, knowing that He sees me, and expecting that, by and by, He will reveal Himself to me. Then He will reveal me and my right intention to misrepresenting men."

That is the first point, beloved: the Lord will come. Settle that in your minds. He will come in His own time, and we are always to be looking for His appearing.

Commanded to Watch for Him

Now, secondly, the Lord bids us to watch for Him. That is the heart of the text: *"Blessed are those servants, whom the lord when he cometh shall find watching."*

Now, what is this watching? Not wishing to use my own words, I thought that I would call your attention to the context. The first essential part of this watching is that we are not to be taken up with present things. You remember that the twenty-second verse speaks of not taking thought about what you will eat or what you will drink; you are not to be absorbed in that. You who are Christians are not to live the fleshly, selfish life that asks, "What will I eat and drink? How can I store up my goods? How can I get food and raiment here?" You are something more than dumb, driven cattle that must think of hay and water. You have immortal spirits. Rise to the dignity of your immortality. Begin to think of the kingdom: the kingdom so soon to come; the kingdom that your Father has given you (Luke 12:32) and that, therefore, you must certainly inherit; the kingdom that Christ has prepared for you, for which He is making you kings and priests unto God (Revelation 1:6) so that you may reign with Him forever.

Be Heavenly Minded

Oh, be not earthbound! Do not cast your anchor here in these troubled waters. Do not build your nest in any of these trees; they are all marked for the axe and are coming down. Your nest will come down, too, if you build it here. *"Set your affection on things above, not on things on the earth"* (Colossians 3:2). Look up yonder,

> Up where eternal ages roll
> Where solid pleasures never die
> And fruits eternal feast the soul.

There project your thoughts and your anxieties, and have a care about the world to come. Be not anxious about the things that pertain to this life.

"Seek ye first the kingdom of God, and his right-eousness; and all these things shall be added unto you" (Matthew 6:33).

Be Ready to Serve

Reading further, you will notice that watching implies keeping ourselves in a serviceable condition: *"Let your loins be girded about..."* (Luke 12:35). You know how the Orientals wear flowing robes, which are always getting in their way. They cannot walk without being tripped up. Thus, if a man has a piece of work at hand, he just tucks in his robe under his girdle, ties his girdle up tightly, and gets ready for the task. Turning the Oriental into the Western figure, we would say in English, "Roll up your shirtsleeves, and prepare for work." That is the way to wait for the Lord, ready for service, so that He may never find you idle when He comes.

Earlier, I described to you a true event in which I interrupted a saintly lady scrubbing her front stoop when I called on her. She was energetically fulfilling her God-given responsibility as keeper of the home. That picture brought forth a desire in my heart to be found by my Master, when He returns, doing the task at hand. May you also desire to be doing your duty. You are to be engaged about those vocations to which God has called you. You are to be doing it all out of love for Christ and as service to Him. Oh, that we might watch in that style, with our loins girded up and doing all for Him (Colossians 3:17)!

Work, wait, and watch! Can you put those three things together? Work, wait, and watch! This is what your Master asks of you. Work, wait, and watch!

Be a Welcoming Light

He would have us wait with our lights burning. If the Master comes home late, let us sit up late for Him. It is not for us to go to bed until He comes home. Have the lights all trimmed; have His chamber well lit up; have the entrance hall ready for His approach. When the King comes, have your torches flaming, so that you may go out to meet the royal Bridegroom and escort Him to His home. If we are to watch for the Lord, it must be with our lamps burning brightly in welcome.

Are you making your light shine among men? Do you think that your conduct and character are examples that will do your neighbors good, and are you trying to teach others the way of salvation? Some professing Christians are like dark lanterns or candles under a bushel (Matthew 5:15). May we never be such! May we stand with our lamps trimmed, our lights burning, and we ourselves as men that wait for their Lord—not walking in darkness, nor concealing our light, but letting it shine brightly!

That is the way to watch for Christ: with your girdle tight about you because you are ready for work, and your lamp flaming out with brightness because you are anxious to illuminate the dark world in which you live.

To put it very plainly, I think that watching for the Lord's Second Coming means acting just as you would like to be acting if He were to come. Recently, I saw in the orphanage classroom that little motto, "What would Jesus do?" That is a very splendid motto for a whole life: "What would Jesus do in such a situation or in this case?" And do just that.

Another good motto for guidance is this: "What would Jesus think of me if He were to come right now?" There are some places into which a Christian should not go because he would not like his Master to find him there. There are some kinds of amusements into which a believer should never enter because he would be ashamed for his Master to come and find him there. There are some conditions of angry temper, pride, petulance, or spiritual sloth in which you would not like to be if you knew that the Master was coming. Suppose an angel's wing should brush your cheek just as you have spoken some unkind word and a voice should say, "Your Master is coming." You would tremble, I am sure, to meet Him in such a condition.

Oh, beloved, let us try every morning to get up as if that were the morning Christ would come. When we go up to bed at night, may we lie down with this thought: "Perhaps I will be awakened by the ringing of the silver trumpets heralding His Coming. Before the sun arises, I may be startled from my dreams by the greatest of all cries, 'The Lord is come! The Lord is come!'" What a check, what an incentive, what a bridle, what a spur, such thoughts as these would be to us! Take this as the guideline for your whole life: Act as if Jesus would return during your performing the deed in which you are engaged; if you would not wish to be caught in that act by the Lord's Coming, quit doing it.

Be a Vigilant Keeper of the Watch

The second verse of our text speaks about the Master coming in the second or the third watch. We are to act as those who keep the watches of the age for Christ. Among the Roman army, it was as it is on board ship: there were certain watches. A Roman soldier stood on guard for three hours; when his watch was completed, another sentry came who took his place. The first man retired and went back to the barracks, and the fresh sentinel stood in his place during his allotted time.

Beloved, we have succeeded a long line of watchmen. Since the days of our Lord when He sent out the chosen twelve to stand upon the citadel and tell how the night waxed or waned, how the watchmen have come and gone! Our God has changed the watchmen, but He has kept the watch. He still sets watchmen on the walls of Zion, who cannot hold their peace day or night, but must watch for the coming of their Master, watch against evil times, watch against error, and watch for the souls of men. At this time, some of us are called to be specially on the watch, and dare we sleep? After such a line of lynx-eyed watchmen, who counted not their lives dear unto them that they might hold their post and watch against the foe, will we be cowards and be afraid, or will we be sluggards and go to our beds? By Him that lives, and was dead, and is alive forevermore (Revelation 1:18), we pray that we may never be guilty of treason to His sacred name and truth. May we watch on to the last moment when the clarion cry will ring out, *"Behold, the bridegroom cometh; go ye out to meet him"* (Matthew 25:6).

Brothers and sisters, you are set to watch tonight just as they did in the brave days of old! Whitefield's and Wesley's men were watchmen, along with those before them in the days of Luther and of Calvin, and back even to the days of our Lord. They kept the watches of the night, and you must do the same until,

> Upstarting at the midnight cry,
> "Behold your heavenly Bridegroom nigh,"

you go forth to welcome your returning Lord.

Be Ready to Welcome Him

We are to wait with one object in view, namely, to open the door to Him and to welcome Him, so *"that when he cometh and knocketh, [we] may open unto him immediately"* (Luke 12:36).

Perhaps you know what it is to go home to a loving, tender wife and children who are watching for you. You have been on a journey, absent for some time; you have written them letters, which they have greatly valued; you have heard from them; but all that is nothing like your personal presence. They are looking for your arrival. If, perchance, your mode of transportation should break down or be late and you arrived at eleven or twelve o'clock at night, you would not expect to find the house all shut up and nobody watching for you. No, you had told them that you would come, and you were quite sure that they would watch for you.

Sometimes I, too, feel rebuked for not watching for my Master, especially when I realize that my dogs are sitting at the door at this very time, waiting for me. Long before I reach home, there they are. At the first sound of the carriage wheels, they lift up their voices with delight because their master is coming home. Oh, if we loved our Lord as dogs love their masters, how we would catch the first sound of His Coming as we are waiting, always waiting, and never truly happy until at last we will see Him! Pardon me for using a dog as a picture of what you ought to be, but when you have attained to a state above that one, I will find another illustration to portray my meaning.

Blessings and Rewards for Watchmen

Now, lastly, there is a reward for those who are watching for Christ's return. Their reward is this: *"Blessed are those servants, whom the lord when he cometh shall find watching."*

Watchmen have a present blessedness. It is a very blessed thing to be on the watch for Christ; it is a blessing to us now. How it detaches you from the world! You can be poor without murmuring; you can be rich without worldliness. You can be sick without sorrowing; you can be healthy without presumption. If you are always waiting for Christ's Coming, untold blessings are wrapped up in that glorious hope. *"Every man that hath this hope in him purifieth himself, even as he is pure"* (1 John 3:3). Blessings are heaped up one upon another in that state of heart in which a man is always looking for his Lord.

But what will be the blessedness when Jesus does come? Well, a part of that blessedness will be in future service. Sunday-school teachers, preachers, and ministers, you must not think that when you are done working here, the Master will say, "I have discharged you from My service. Go, sit on a heavenly mount, and sing yourselves away forever and ever." Never!

I am only learning how to preach now; I will be able to preach by and by. You are just learning to teach now; soon you will be able to teach. To angels, principalities, and powers, you will make known the manifold wisdom of God. I sometimes aspire to the thought of a congregation of angels and archangels who will sit and wonder as I tell what God has done for me. I will be to them an everlasting monument of the grace of God to an unworthy wretch, upon whom He looked with infinite compassion and saved with a wonderful salvation.

All those stars, those worlds of light, who knows how many of them are inhabited? I believe there are regions beyond imagination to which every child of God will become an everlasting illumination, a living example of the love of God in Christ Jesus. The people in those far-distant lands could not see Calvary as this world has seen it, but they will hear of it from the redeemed. Remember how the Lord will say, *"Well done, thou good and faithful servant: thou hast been faithful over a few things, I will make thee ruler over many things"* (Matthew 25:21). The servant is to keep on doing something, you see. Instead of having some little bit of a village to govern, he is to be made ruler over some great province. So it is in this passage.

Reading further in Luke, we find: *"Of a truth I say unto you, that he will make him ruler over all that he hath"* (Luke 12:44). That is, the man who has been a faithful and wise steward of God here will be called of God to more eminent service hereafter. If a person serves his Master well, when his Master comes, He will promote him to still higher service.

Do you not know how it used to be in the Spartan army? Here is a man who has fought well and been a splendid soldier. He is covered with wounds on his chest. The next time there is a war, they say, "Poor fellow, we will reward him! He will lead the way in the first battle. He fought so well before when he met one hundred with a little troop behind him; now, he can meet ten thousand with a much larger troop." "Oh," you object, "that is giving him more work!"

That is God's way of rewarding His people, and a blessed thing it is for the industrious servant. His rest is in serving God with all his might.

This will be our heaven, not to go there to roost, but to be always on the wing, forever flying and forever resting at the same time. They *"do his commandments, hearkening unto the voice of his word"* (Psalm 103:20). *"His servants shall serve him: And they shall see his face"* (Revelation 22:3–4). Blended together, these two things make a noble ambition for every Christian.

May the Lord keep you waiting, working, and watching so that when He comes, you may have the blessedness of entering upon some larger, higher, nobler service than you could accomplish now, for which you are preparing by the lowlier and more arduous service of this world! God bless you, beloved.

If any of you do not know my Lord, and therefore do not look for His appearing, remember that He will come whether you look for Him or not. When He comes, you will have to stand at His bar. One of the events that will follow His Coming will be your being summoned before His judgment seat. How will you answer Him then? How will you answer Him if you have refused His love and turned a deaf ear to the invitations of His mercy? If you have delayed and delayed and delayed, how will you answer Him? How will you answer Him in that day if you stand speechless? Your silence will condemn you, and the King will say, *"Bind him hand and foot, and take him away, and cast him into outer darkness"* (Matthew 22:13).

May God grant that we may believe in the Lord Jesus unto life eternal, and then wait for His appearing from heaven, for His love's sake! Amen.